A New Hope for Mexico

A New Hope for Mexico

Saying No to Corruption, Violence, and Trump's Wall

Andrés Manuel López Obrador

Translated by Natascha Uhlmann

OR Books
London · New York

Published by OR Books, New York and London
Visit our website at www.orbooks.com

All rights information: rights@orbooks.com

First printing 2018

First published in 2017 as *2018: La Salida* and *Oye, Trump* by Editorial
Planeta Mexicana.

Cataloging-in-Publication data is available from the Library of Congress.
A catalog record for this book is available from the British Library.

Typeset by Lapiz Digital Services, Chennai, India.
Published for the book trade by OR Books in partnership with
Counterpoint Press.
Distributed to the trade by Publishers Group West.

ISBN 978-1-944869-85-4 paperback
ISBN 978-1-944869-86-1 ebook

CONTENTS

TRANSLATOR AND EDITOR'S NOTE

Natascha Uhlmann

This work first appeared as two separate books, both published in Spanish in 2017: *Oye, Trump* (a collection of López
Obrador's speeches in defense of migrants) and *La Salida* (*The Exit*,
a broader political platform addressing economic ills, migration,
and corruption). Although each of these books provide insight into
the man who—according to many—will likely be the next president of Mexico—they are in many ways even more powerful when
combined: AMLO's policy proposals underpin and flesh out his
more short-form work, while his impassioned speeches make clear
the stakes of his more detailed political roadmap.

That, too, is the central takeaway of AMLO's work—together,
we are more than the sum of our parts. This work is a powerful
call for solidarity, presenting a tangible way forward in the face of
endemic corruption and anti-migrant rhetoric. Rosa Luxemburg
once remarked: "The more that social democracy develops, grows,
and becomes stronger, the more the enlightened masses of workers
will take their own destinies, the leadership of their movement, and
the determination of its direction into their own hands." In this
book, López Obrador elucidates the steps which are needed for real
and lasting change to transform Mexico, systemically, culturally,
and institutionally.

A few decisions should be noted: Mexican pesos were con-
verted to USD at the conversion rate in effect in April 2018. Some

words that are inseparable from the Mexican context were left in their original Spanish, followed by an English approximation.

My deepest thanks to Steven Clarry, Donald and Maria Uhlmann, and Colin Robinson for their invaluable support and encouragement.

NYC, April 2018

INTRODUCTION

In these pages I want to explain why I regard corruption as Mexico's central problem. At the same time, I want to call upon all Mexicans—men and women, rich and poor, city and town folk, believers and atheists—to reach a national consensus that places honesty as a central principle for both the people and government. I will explain the ways in which the country has been looted, and I will discuss how neoliberal—or what I refer to as *Neoporfirista*[1]— politics has given rise to rampant inequality, shocking poverty, frustration, resentment, hate, and violence.

I'm not going to limit myself here to condemning corruption and calling for its eradication; I also want to set out ways to combat it and move toward a new politics, a different economic model, and the strengthening of cultural, moral, and spiritual values that can revitalize our nation.

Although we're not presenting the full Alternative Nation Project[2] until closer to the 2018 election, I will share some of its central points here, plans which are being developed by experts in their respective fields: governing by example, weeding out corruption, denying anyone the right to be above the law, managing public resources responsibly, and investing in the nation's prosperity.

---

1   A return to widespread corruption and repression characterized by the rule of Porfirio Díaz in the late nineteenth and early twentieth centuries.

2   López Obrador's political platform.

1

With this new and honest model of political action, there will be no need to raise taxes or continue to increase the public debt. Living and working conditions will improve, as economic and spiritual well-being flourish. In sum, we will achieve the *pueblo*'s prosperity and the rebirth of Mexico, as General Francisco J. Múgica[3] said, "through sheer morality and a few minor reforms."

I hope that these ideas become a reality, and I am working toward that end, but whatever happens, the program I am setting out here is dedicated to the younger generations, with the understanding that if we can't create a new Mexico today because contemporary society won't allow it, they, our youth, must take on this necessary task.

Although we followed the 2016 US elections closely, the principles of nonintervention and state sovereignty led us to keep a respectful distance from its internal politics, and the few times we did offer an opinion, we did so without interfering or taking sides.

But there are some things that can't go unacknowledged. I recall that Donald Trump, upon announcing his candidacy on June 16, 2015, commented, "When Mexico sends its people, they're not sending their best. They're not sending you. They send people that have lots of problems, and they're bringing those problems with us. They're bringing drugs, they're bringing crime, they're rapists."

We've since asked ourselves whether Trump truly didn't understand the basis of mass immigration or if he was just resorting to demagoguery, because Mexico does not "send" anyone to the United States; it happens that millions of people have left our country in the pursuit of a better life through honest work in our neighbor to the north. The majority have left to improve their economic situation, while others flee the violence that plagues our homeland.

After the election, when the Republican contender was sworn into office, we decided to act. We knew that the current Mexican president, Enrique Peña Nieto, would not meet his duty to represent Mexico with dignity and that he would be unwilling to vigorously defend migrants. Experience proved us correct.

---

3   A Mexican revolutionary who later went on to govern Tabasco and Michoacán.

As campaign rhetoric morphed into government policy, we could no longer stand by idly. Our first move was to participate in a meeting on January 20, 2017, the day of Donald Trump's inauguration, with the people in the border town of Acuña, Coahuila. Subsequently, in a two month span, we attended public gatherings in Los Angeles, Chicago, El Paso, Phoenix, New York, Washington, San Francisco, and Laredo.

As part of that mobilization, we delivered a note of protest to the United Nations, and a complaint to the Inter-American Commission on Human Rights about Trump's effort to build a border wall between Mexico and the United States, and about his attempts to persecute migrant workers.

The fact of the matter is that many Americans feel uneasy about the status of their neighbor to the south. We appreciate their concerns. At the same time, we want to clarify the reasons behind migration from Mexico, and initiate a dialogue with sectors of the American populace which have been subject to a misinformation campaign unleashed against Mexicans and migrants.

My central thesis is this: our migrants and our country deserve better.

I want to thank Rogelio Ramírez de la O for his reflections on economics and data. I also want to acknowledge the support of Father Alejandro Solalinde, who accompanied us to Los Angeles, and Elenita Poniatowska, who was with us in Laredo, where she read out the epilogue that concludes this book. Finally, I wish to thank Jaime Avilés, Jesús Ramírez Cuevas, Pedro Miguel, and Laura González Nieto for their help in revising this work.

¡Oye, Trump! Speech 1

The Night of the Election

A message to the people of Mexico on the US election results.

I believe it's important to address the Mexican people, foremost migrant workers and their families, but also all of the people of Mexico, including businessmen and investors:

There is no cause for concern at the US election results. Don't forget that Mexico, through the hard work and sacrifice of our forefathers, is a free, independent and sovereign nation, not a colony or protectorate; we are beholden to no foreign government. Be at peace. I believe that it was wrong of Mexico's political elites to take sides in the election; they have forgotten the principles of nonintervention and the right of the people to self-determination. In any case, we will find strength through our unity in the face of any eventuality.

I call on the Mexican people to be at peace. We will forge ahead; there are no problems we can't address because we will assert our right to sovereignty, whoever may occupy the White House.

I repeat: Mexico is a free, independent, and sovereign nation.

Without sabre rattling, we will assert our independence and our right to sovereignty.

We have nothing to fear. We shall forge ahead.

CHAPTER 1

A GANG OF THUGS

Iopen with a categorical assertion: Mexico's crisis cannot be confronted without first addressing corruption and and the failure to prosecute people benefiting from it, which requires regime change and the establishment of a new political order, one that is democratic, that promotes the rule of law, that is humanist and distinctively honest. The Republic that exists today is a republic in name only, not a government by the *pueblo* and for the *pueblo*. The State has come to serve a rapacious minority and, as Tolstoy once wrote, a state that does not procure justice is no more than a pack of miscreants. This definition, that of a writer, not a pundit or theorist, has clarity and simplicity and comes closest to our present political reality. In Mexico the governing class constitutes a gang of plunderers that operate throughout the country. This may seem like an exaggeration, and one might argue that it's always been this way, but the astounding dishonesty of the neoliberal period (from 1983 to present) is wholly unprecedented. It constitutes a qualitative shift in the disintegration of the country.

The system has been utterly corrupted. The political and economic powers feed off each other, and the theft of public goods has become their *modus operandi*. Corruption is no longer a matter of a few isolated instances, but a systematic practice. In the so-called stabilizing development period (1930s–80s), the government dared not privatize communal lands, forests, beaches, railroads, mines,

electricity, and petroleum above all; in this bitter period of neoliberalism, they have dedicated themselves, as in the *Porfiriato*[4]
period, to handing over our firms and territory and public goods,
and even functions of the State, to domestic and foreign entities.
It's no longer about individual acts of dereliction, nor a web of
complicity at the expense of the public; now, feeding corruption
has become the principal function of the State.

The politics of pillage—more specifically, the neoliberal
model—is a set of dogmas and mantras asserting that privatization
is the cure-all, the sole and perfect fix to the country's economic
and social issues. Though it may seem redundant, the *Dictionary of
the Royal Spanish Academy* states that privatization means to make
what is public private. Quite literally, "Transferring a business or
public good to the private sector." The heralds of neoliberalism call
upon all sorts of falsehoods to justify this sacking. They exalt the
myth of market supremacy; they assert that sovereignty is irrelevant in the face of globalization, that the State need not promote
development or redistribute wealth, because wealth spreads when
the elites prosper. But this is sophistry, because wealth isn't water
and doesn't trickle down. Neoliberal propagandists have gone so
far as to resurrect the old *Porfirista* wisdom that there will always
be a wealthy elite, living in stark contrast to the vast majority,
and even with every absurd justification at their disposal they still
shirk responsibility for the State's failure to provide for the people.
Denying any right to justice, they condemn those born into poverty
to die in poverty.

As neoliberalism spreads across the globe, this supposed "new
paradigm" has been used as armor behind which to plunder the country on a scale never before seen. The Washington Consensus took
shape under Miguel de la Madrid's administration (1982–88), but its
grasp was strengthened under his successor, Carlos Salinas de Gortari
(1988–94). During this period we saw the beginnings of a new legal
framework, one that legalized pillage behind a rhetoric of selling off

4   A reference to Porfirio Díaz, dictator who served seven terms as president of
    Mexico (1877–1880 and 1884–1911).

inefficiently run government entities. Though formally privatization bids were supposed to take place under the guise of fairness and transparency, it was clear from the start who the winners would be. One need only recall that Salinas, his brother Raúl, and the secretary of finance, Pedro Aspe, benefitted from this distribution of banks and other assets that had previously belonged to Mexico.

Thus, in thirteen months—from June 1991 to July 1992—and with an average of twenty business days per bank, 18 lending institutions were shuttered. In a mere five years—December 1988 to December of 1993—251 businesses were privatized, including Telmex, Mexicana de Aviación, Televisión Azteca, Siderúrgica Lázaro Cárdenas, Altos Hornos de México, Astilleros Unidos de Veracruz, Fertilizantes Mexicanos, as well as insurance providers, sugar mills, mines, and factories. The transfer of public goods to a select few wasn't limited to banks and state-owned entities. Communal lands were also privatized, as were highways, ports, and airports. And with that, domestic and foreign business opportunities increased significantly for Pemex[5] and the Federal Electricity Commission.

The economic system imposed under Salinas was perpetuated under Ernesto Zedillo, Vicente Fox, and Felipe Calderón, and the beneficiaries of Salinas's spoils continued to accumulate not only wealth but political influence. Before long they became a political power in and of themselves, a power that operated beyond the reach of constitutionally bound institutions. It is these figures who determine the fate of our most pressing political questions of the day—the questions fiercely debated in the Chamber of Deputies and the Senate; in the Supreme Court; the National Electoral Institute and Electoral Tribune; by the Attorney General; the Secretary of Finance; and the PRI and PAN[6]. What's more, they enjoy unfettered control of the media.

---

5   Short for Petroleos Mexicanos (Mexican Petroleum), central to the Mexican economy (and Latin America's second largest enterprise).

6   Institutional Revolutionary Party (PRI) and National Action Party (PAN), Mexico's center-right parties.

These tycoons, quite understandably, are betting on the continuation of this state of affairs and have forestalled regime change through bribes and manipulation. A fruit of these efforts was the installation of Enrique Peña Nieto as president of Mexico. He's one more puppet for the elite, a frivolous and irrelevant character. And yet this spineless, immoral, unpredictable sycophant has led the deterioration of the country in every facet of public life. Not only are we plagued by impoverishment and unemployment, but instability and insecurity are rampant. Decadence prospered because a new collective politics was not pursued; the regime instead doubled down on its grasp of neoliberal politics. In a mere two years Peña Nieto managed to impose a foreign agenda on a compliant populace. As Mexico's elites conspired, so-called "reforms" were enacted in the spheres of labor, education, economic policy, and energy. The country's sovereignty and the *pueblo*'s integrity were violated, leaving frustration, chaos, and violence in their wake.

¡Oye, Trump! Speech 2

The First Day of Trump's Presidency

Acuña City, Coahuila, January 20, 2017

Today, Donald Trump took office as president of the United States and launched yet another attack against those he considers foreigners, both at home and abroad.

I regret this uncomfortable new reality, but I don't rule out the possibility of things improving for the sake of both our nations.

Our task is to try and persuade Trump, but at the same time, we must create the conditions to make him listen to reason.

Before the US elections, we were prudent and did not publicly favor any candidate or party; we held firmly to the principles of nonintervention and self-determination, but now we cannot stand idly by as US foreign policy seeks to encroach on the dignity and legitimate interests of the Mexican people.

What Trump expressed in his message a few hours ago represents a significant setback in US foreign policy and a vulgar threat to human rights.

Who could forget that, a century ago, President Woodrow Wilson was the main arbiter of peace negotiations following the First World War? He created the League of Nations, the precursor to the United Nations, to foster brotherhood among people and to resolve problems through agreement, not force.

Who could set aside, as was proposed in Washington today, the four fundamental human rights declared by President Franklin Delano Roosevelt:

1. Freedom of expression
2. Freedom of worship
3. Freedom from want
4. Freedom from fear

Who could transform, overnight, a country that so sympathized with the migrants of the world into a spiritual wasteland, a state of abuse, oppression, and expulsion, a state that denies justice to those who seek to escape poverty through hard work? What happens then to the idea of fellowship for all?

This is why we shall act to defend the human rights of our countrymen—and of migrants around the world. This entails fighting against the creation of a wall, against deportations, and against unilateral and tyrannical decisions in the realm of trade.

This is our Action Plan to address the menace unleashed today:

1. Request that Mexican president Peña Nieto arrange an emergency meeting with the US president today, to take a personal stand for human rights and our national interest.
2. Convert Mexican consulates in the US into migrant defense offices.
3. Take prompt and effective action to confront this menace. We have the right to put forward our agenda. We don't seek to meet arrogance with bravado, nor retell a David and Goliath story; we seek merely to assert our sovereignty, acting always with courage and conviction.
4. Roll out a national emergency plan to confront the protectionist policies announced by Donald Trump.
5. This plan must consider, among other approaches, bolstering our national production and strengthening our internal markets to create jobs in Mexico; investing in the construction industry; using our energy sector as a lever for national development; and constructing refineries to avoid having to purchase gas and other energy sources from abroad. We must also provide support to our rural areas and protect our producers by setting guaranteed prices for crops and basic foods (corn, beans, rice, wheat, milk, chicken, eggs, and beef, among others). We aim to achieve food self-sufficiency, producing what we consume.
6. Promote a bilateral agreement with Canada to increase the employment of Mexican workers there and to secure a greater investment in Canadian mining companies in Mexico, paying workers a living wage and respecting the laws that protect our environment.

7. Support the needs (investment, commerce, job creation) of our border towns along the 1,800 mile shared border with the US. This must include lowering taxes, reducing the cost of gasoline, diesel, gas and electricity, and moving our customs office twelve miles inland from the border. Regarding the possible modification of tariffs and tax increases on exporters to the US, we must consider a duty-free zone that will benefit Mexican border towns.

8. Diversify economic and commercial relationships. We must accept that we can't put all of our eggs in one basket. We must promote investment, financing, and commerce with countries across the globe.

9. Mount appeals to international authorities, such as the World Trade Organization (WTO), in the event of arbitrary tax and customs modifications that would disadvantage companies based in Mexico.

10. Establish a responsible budget to finance our national emergency plan. We project savings of 360 billion pesos (US$19 billion) through the eradication of corruption and the elimination of the inflated privileges of high ranking officials.

One cannot fix an injustice from the outside. We must reach out to the hard-working American people and confront this anti-immigrant propaganda. It must not take root, neither in small towns nor in large cities.

We shall strive tirelessly to convince the US government that fellowship, without walls or borders, is the best approach.

Without impinging on the rights of others, we will firmly defend our freedom and sovereignty.

CHAPTER 2
PRIVATIZATION IS THEFT

In terms of our collective well-being, the politics of pillage has been an unmitigated disaster. In economic and social affairs, we've been regressing instead of moving forward. But this is hardly surprising: the model itself is *designed* to favor a small minority of corrupt politicians and white collar criminals. The model does not seek to meet the needs of the people, or to avoid violence and conflict; it seeks neither to govern openly nor honestly. It seeks to monopolize the bureaucratic apparatus and transfer public goods to private hands, making claims that this will somehow bring about prosperity.

The result: monstrous economic and social inequality. Mexico is one of the countries with the greatest disparities between wealth and poverty in the world. According to a 2015 article written by Gerardo Esquivel, a professor at the College of Mexico and a Harvard graduate, 10 percent of Mexicans control 64.4 percent of the national income, and 1 percent own 21 percent of the country's wealth. But most significantly, inequality in Mexico deepened precisely during the neoliberal period. Privatization allowed it to thrive.

It's also important to make note of the following statistic: in July 1988, when Carlos Salinas was imposed as president on the Mexican people through electoral fraud, only one Mexican family sat on the *Forbes* list of the world's richest people—the Garza Sada family, with $2 billion to their name. By the end of Salinas's term in office, twenty-four Mexicans had joined the list, owning a combined total of US$44.1 billion. Nearly all had made off with companies, mines, and banks belonging to the people of Mexico. In 1988, Mexico sat at 26th place on a list of countries with the most billionaires; by 1994, Mexico was in fourth place, just beneath the United States, Japan, and Germany.

The starkest proof of soaring inequality in the neoliberal period is provided by the same financial institutions that have promoted this model. That's why it's useful to take a look at the graphic that Esquivel presents in his study, with numbers from the World Bank and the Organisation for Economic Co-operation and Development (OECD).

As is readily observed, economic inequality today is greater than it was in the 1980s, and perhaps greater than the periods before, though a lack of accurate records makes such comparisons difficult. Although Esquivel doesn't highlight it, in the graphic we see the extent to which inequality skyrocketed during Salinas's term, when the transfer of public goods to private hands was at its most intense. Under Salinas, the divide between rich and poor deepened like never before. Salinas is the godfather of modern inequality in Mexico.

It's clear, then, that privatization is not the panacea that its proponents would have us believe. If it were, beneficial effects would by now be visible. At this juncture it's fair to ask neoliberalism's supporters: How have Mexicans benefited from the privatization of the telecommunications system? Is it a mere coincidence that, in terms of price and quality, both phone and internet service in Mexico rank 70th worldwide, far below other members of the OECD? What social benefits has the media monopoly conferred— other than to its direct beneficiaries, who have amassed tremendous wealth in exchange for protecting the corrupt regime, through brazenly slanted coverage of opposition candidates? What have we gained through the privatization of *Ferrocarriles Nacionales*[7] in 1995, if twenty-two years later these outside investors haven't built

---

7   Mexico's state-owned railroad company.

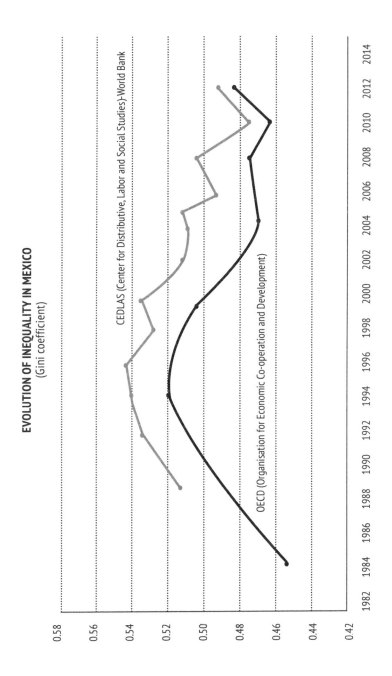

EVOLUTION OF INEQUALITY IN MEXICO
(Gini coefficient)

CEDLAS (Center for Distributive, Labor and Social Studies)-World Bank

OECD (Organisation for Economic Co-operation and Development)

new train lines, and can charge whatever they want for transport? How have we benefited from the leasing out of 240 million acres, 40 percent of the country (Mexico has 482 million acres total) for the extraction of gold, silver, and copper? Mexican miners earn, on average, sixteen times less than those in the United States and Canada. Companies in this field have extracted in five short years as much gold and silver as the Spanish Empire took in three centuries. Most outrageously, up until recently they were extracting these minerals untaxed. In short, we are living through the greatest pillage of natural resources in Mexico's history.

This destructive policy has done nothing for the country. Statistics show that in the past thirty years we've failed to advance. To the contrary, in terms of economic growth we've fallen behind even an impoverished country like Haiti. The only constant has been economic stagnation and unemployment, which has forced millions of Mexicans to migrate or to make a living through the informal economy, if not resorting to crime. Half of the population is precariously employed with no safety net. The widespread abandonment of agriculture, lack of job or educational prospects for our youth, and spiraling unemployment has resulted in insecurity and violence that have taken millions of lives. In the magazine *Mundo Ejecutivo*, Alejandro Desfassiaux reports that "the INEGI[8] and the RNPED[9] reported over 175,000 homicides and 26,798 instances of missing people between 2006–2015." As Desfassiaux puts it, "this violence affected countless others when family members are included."[10]

For these reasons, it's illogical to think we can end corruption through the same neoliberal political and economic approach that has so patently failed in the past. To the contrary, until there's a deep and sustained change, Mexico will continue its decline. Our present course is unsustainable, and we are nearing the point of

8   National Institute of Statistics and Geography.

9   National Registry of Disappeared or Lost Persons.

10 Alejandro Desfassiaux, *37 meses sin respuestas*. *Mundo Ejecutivo* (January 2016), 52.

complete collapse. Our political economy today echoes the failures of the *Porfiriato* period at the end of the nineteenth century, when the prosperity of a few was placed above the needs of the many. That failed experiment culminated in armed revolution. The need to topple the PRIAN[11] oligarchy and their ilk has never been greater, just as happened with Porfirio Díaz. But this time around we will not descend into violence, acting rather through a revolution of conscience, through an awakening and an organization of the *pueblo* to rid Mexico of the corruption that consumes it. In short: instead of the neoliberal agenda, which consists of the appropriation for the few, we must create a new consensus that prioritizes honesty as a way of living and governing, and regains the great material, social, and moral wealth that was once Mexico's. We should never forget the words of José María Morelos[12] two hundred years ago: "Alleviate both indigency and extravagance." We must ensure that the democratic state, through legal means, distributes Mexico's wealth equitably, subject to the premise that equal treatment cannot exist without equal access, and that justice consists of giving more to he or she who has less.

11   This expression refers to two parties, the PRI and the PAN, the implication being that they're one and the same.

12   A revolutionary who played a leading role in the Mexican War of Independence.

¡Oye, Trump! Speech 3

Blessed Migration

Los Angeles, California, February 12, 2017

Since time immemorial the migrant has been both vilified and vindicated across the globe. The Bible asserts: "Thou shalt not oppress the laborer that is poor and needy, whether he be of thy brethren, or of thy strangers that are in thy land within thy gates" (Deuteronomy 24:14). As history shows, however, this principle is rarely upheld. The persecution of migrants has become a powerful political tool. It is through this lens that we must interpret current events in the United States.

The ardent anti-immigrant campaign was not motivated by economics; it is a fundamentally ideological program. One group benefits greatly from sowing nationalist discord.

To be clear, people are right to be concerned with unemployment and low wages; indeed, Germans had a healthy fear of inflation before Hitler's arrival.[13] But blaming inflation—or any other hardship—on specific social or cultural groups has clear political consequences.

Donald Trump and his inner circle have effectively stirred up anti-immigrant sentiment, particularly against people of Mexican origin.

This hateful rhetoric allowed him to win the presidency. His administration expects to preserve its power by inciting hatred and pitting the people against one another.

We must not underestimate the intelligence of these US politicians. They are not fools. Trump's belligerent rhetoric follows a cold and calculated political strategy. The propaganda he churns out derives from the theory of *Lebensraum*[14] in the face of so-called foreign enemies, and the promoting of aggressive nationalism.

---

13 Stefan Zweig, in *The World of Yesterday*, wrote: "One must recall always that nothing exasperated the German people, nothing made it so maniacal with hate, so ripe for Hitler, as inflation."

14 An ideological concept that proliferated in Nazi Germany asserting the need for colonized territory for a State to flourish.

Throughout the presidential campaign, the effectiveness of this political strategy was not fully understood. And as such, it was not countered. But there is still time to address the root problems and minimize the harm caused. We can start by recognizing that fear of "the outsider" has taken a dangerous hold.

A few days ago, the media covered an American couple who had dinner in a Texas restaurant, and left a note on the receipt reading: "The food was delicious and service was great, but the owner is Mexican, so we won't be back," closing with Trump's now famous "America First."

The calculating and irresponsible neo-fascist administration would build walls that reduce the United States to an enormous ghetto and equate Mexicans in general, and our migrants in particular, with the stigmatized and persecuted Jews in Hitler's era.

Faced with such prejudice, protests are not enough. Our most urgent task is to reach out to the American people. We must confront this hateful campaign and resist any threats to our fundamental human rights. We must focus our attention on linking up with good-willed Americans—of whom there are many—who are victims of this manipulation and deceit. We must focus on those in small cities and towns, those with strong civic, moral, and spiritual values that are being poisoned by hate for migrant workers.

Recall that Trump won 2,626 counties, while Hillary Clinton won a mere 487, although these counties encompassed 64 percent of America's economic activity. Trump preyed on the hopes of the impoverished, giving them a convenient scapegoat for their economic malaise.

But those in small counties were disproportionately affected by the 2008 recession. These counties have not yet seen economic recovery, have not recovered lost jobs, while in recent years new jobs have focused largely on the service sector in large metropolitan areas, where Latino, Asian, and African American workers are more frequently employed.

It's urgent to reach out to these populations most affected by the economic recession. We must explain to them the root cause of the crisis that is hitting them; we must help them understand that if they lack jobs, good salaries, and well-being, migrants are not to blame; rather, it is a result of poor governance that penalizes those below and benefits the wealthy. We must explain, for example, that during the 2008 crisis it was large financial institutions that were saved first. We must talk about unequal wealth distribution and the fact that the rich contribute very little to taxes while the less well-off shoulder a disproportionate burden.

We must remind them that the biggest factories in Mexico were set up by American investors and businessmen who export merchandise and profits to the United States, leaving workers behind with meager benefits and paying virtually nil in taxes, and that while the use of automation in these factories may have led to huge increases in production, there have been no increases in hiring.

The fostering of an economy for the elites has not led to job creation or development. Trump often claims that the United States buys more than it sells to Mexico, that there is a formal deficit of US$60 billion. But this is only a partial truth. Why? Because our exports contain a high percentage of US capital, technology, and components.

Phrased differently, if it were true that NAFTA solely benefitted Mexico, our economy would not continue to stagnate nor would we have such sustained migration rates. In 1970, when Mexican exports were only at 7.8 percent of GDP, economic growth was at 6.5 percent, whereas now, as exports have reached 35.3 percent of GDP, our economy has only grown by 2.5 percent. We are not growing significantly; although we export goods of great value, we also import most of those inputs in the first place.

We must present these and other arguments to the American people. Through reasoned discussions we can convince those most affected that it is possible to create a better society on both sides of the border without hate or resentment when we work together, in good faith, toward justice.

We must set aside hostility. Respect, understanding, and cooperation are more beneficial to both sides.

We thus call upon American academics, intellectuals, and individuals with civic, social, and democratic values to help us develop a plan to persuade workers and America's middle classes that migrants are not their enemies but rather their kin, decent human beings who, much like the founders of their great nation, were forced to leave their homes and start anew.

We must counter Trump's rhetoric rationally, not by stooping to his level but through reasoned and dignified arguments. We must engage on the battleground of ideas. We will fight against egotism, we will fight in defense of the vulnerable, such that they may not be resented for their class, nationality, or religion. We will meet hateful rhetoric with the spiritual principle of love for one's neighbor.

Inciting hatred against migrants is an attack on our shared humanity.

Our ancestors left Africa, reached the Middle East and Europe, populated Asia and ultimately arrived here.

Migration is the cornerstone of nations, and this great country is an example. The strength of any culture rests with the sum of its influences, its tongues, and its thought.

Humans have populated nearly the entire planet, yet we all come from the same cradle. Today, we recognize our shared history through universal fellowship.

This is why, when one builds a wall to segregate populations, or when the word "foreigner" is used to denigrate and discriminate against a people, it is an insult to humanity, intelligence, and history.

Neither the wall nor jingoistic rhetoric can withstand the talent and dignity of the American people. Through rational argumentation, the strength of public opinion will force those who, like Donald Trump, are predisposed to sabre rattling, to open their eyes and to see reason.

Here, in the state of California, a blessed refuge for migrants, we recall César Chávez, an exceptional warrior for social justice who taught us that liberty is not asked for—it is taken. Here, in Los

Angeles, we want you, the Mexican people on this side of the border, to know that we are with you and that we are one.

As Martin Luther King Jr. said: "Darkness cannot drive out darkness; only light can do that. Hate cannot drive out hate; only love can do that."

CHAPTER 3
VORACIOUS NEPOTISM

Corruption isn't limited to the handover of public goods to lobbyists and those who employ them; it's also at play in the allocation of public works contracts and the taking over of state functions. Cronyism is a hallmark of a corrupt state. It has plagued Mexico since the rule of Porfirio Díaz. Back then, the Englishman Weetman Pearson was awarded generous contracts to build the Grand Canal of Mexico City, the ports of Veracruz, Coatzacoalcos and Salina Cruz, and the train tracks for Istmo de Tehuantepec; he was also granted rights to extract oil throughout the country. In return, the dictator's son, Porfirio Díaz Ortega, handled petroleum and asphalt sales for the company, and the "honest tyrant" lived comfortably in exile from the stocks he owned in Pearson's company, among his many other sources of income.

After the fall of the dictatorship, conducting business at the expense of the state became standard practice. There were honorable exceptions, such as General Francisco J. Múgica, who governed Tabasco for a mere ten months and twenty days in 1915; he received "the treasury at a deficit of 126,000 pesos and left it with a surplus of 120,582 pesos." This general from Michoacán, who had been a seminarian before becoming a military man, reflected: "From whence this boon of relative prosperity from a bankrupt treasury? Through sheer morality and a few minor reforms."[15]

---

15 Antonio Elías Balcázar, *Tabasco en sepia. Economía y sociedad, 1880–1940* (México: Universidad Juárez Autónoma de Tabasco, 2003), 222.

Around the same time, Múgica sent an emotive letter to Salvador Alvarado, governor of Yucatan whom he admired greatly. "Please give me your guidance, general." A few lines below, he lamented the "dreadful cabals" that obtained contracts through friendships with the men close to Venustiano Carranza.

In 1923, during the corrupt rule of Álvaro Obregon,[16] one revolutionary noted that of Mexico's twenty-eight governors, only two were honest. He reasoned: "The best one can hope for is not a governor who won't enrich himself through the position, since they nearly all do. What we hope for is one who does something for his state in between bouts of ransacking. Most take everything they can and leave nothing behind."[17]

The historian John W. F. Dulles opens his book *Yesterday in Mexico* with a reference to Obregon's tale of how he lost his arm in the battle of Celaya facing down Villa's troops: his men scoured the area searching for his severed arm, until a close friend who "knew him intimately" took from his bag a glittering piece of gold, after which they "witnessed a miracle: the arm came flying out from its hiding place and lovingly took the coin between its fingertips. It was the only way to find my missing arm."[18]

In his great 1958 novel, *Where the Air is Clear,* Carlos Fuentes writes of a northern revolutionary named Robles who arrives in Mexico City and, armed with insider information, buys up plots of land that will soon benefit from urban investments in infrastructure. Selling the land at a profit, Robles goes from speculator to banker and amasses a large fortune. More recently, Gonzalo N. Santos, Lord of San Luis Potosí, writes in his autobiography that

---

16 A general in the Mexican Revolution who went on to become the president of Mexico from 1920–24.

17 Roger D. Hansen, *La política del desarrollo mexicano* (México: Siglo xxi Editores, 2007), 166.

18 Obregon here facetiously refers to his reputation for corruption. John W. F. Dulles, *Ayer en México. Una crónica de la Revolución (1919–1936)* (México: Fondo de Cultura Económica, 1977), 11.

"the fruit of the tree of 'morals' is worth jack shit."[19] Meanwhile, Carlos Hank González popularized the phrase "A poor politician is a *poor* politician."

The scope of today's corruption is wholly unprecedented. The brazen politicians of the past don't hold a candle to Carlos Salinas[20] and his ilk. Enrique Peña Nieto outdoes them all. His cozy relationships with government contractors are numerous, although he does have his favorites: one example is Juan Armando Hinojosa's Grupo Higa company, in Reynosa, Tamaulipas.

Hinojosa was first linked to Peña Nieto when the latter governed the State of Mexico. Ever since, he's been Peña Nieto's favorite contractor. Here's an anecdote: when I was mayor of Mexico City, in 2004, we built the Dr. Belisario Domínguez Specialist Hospital in the borough of Iztapalapa. It had 150 beds and cost 350 million pesos (US$18.8 million). At around the same time, during Peña Nieto's term as governor of the State of Mexico, he contracted Grupo Higa to build a hospital in the municipality of Zumpango. A facility with 125 beds ended up costing 7 billion pesos (US$377 million); that is to say, twenty times more than the facility in Iztapalapa. Beyond this staggering discrepancy, the facility was more expensive still due to the financing plan selected. The State of Mexico's secretary of finance, Luis Videgaray, approved a contract granting Hinojosa 282 million pesos (US$15 million) per year in interest for a period of twenty-five years. This scheme, known as PPS (Projects to Provide Services) was an initiative of the Calderón government.[21] These public-private partnerships have led to the bankruptcy of multiple local governments.

Corruption and cronyism were again evident in the construction of a 225-bed hospital in Ixtapaluca, Mexico that cost 7.5 billion pesos (US$404 million). The company that built it is owned by

---

19   In Spanish this is a delightful play on the words *moral* and *mora* (blackberry tree). This phrase refers to the idea that morals are useless in politics.

20   Carlos Salinas, former Mexican president who became embroiled in corruption scandals.

21   Former Mexican president Felipe Calderón served from 2006–2012.

Hipólito Gerard Rivero, the brother-in-law of both Carlos Salinas and José Antonio González Anaya.[22] It's important to note that at the time of this business arrangement—during Calderón's rule—Salinas's brother-in-law was serving as Ernesto Cordero's operator in his role as deputy finance minister. Under Peña Nieto's rule, his political connections secured him a position first as director of the Social Security Institute, and now as a director of Pemex. Calderón's reign was a highly profitable one for Cordero, González Anaya, and the secretary of finance, José Antonio Meade, all three of whom were intimately involved in engineering this funding mechanism.

Under Peña Nieto, the State of Mexico assigned Hinojosa contracts worth 23 billion pesos (US$1.2 billion) with the complicity of then public works minister Gerardo Ruiz Esparza, who today serves as the secretary of communications and transport. When Peña Nieto came to power, Ruiz Esparza quickly became a man of influence, and the contracts granted to Hinojosa grew exponentially. Among the most notorious was the planned construction of the express train from Querétaro to Mexico City, with an estimated budget of 58 billion pesos (US$3.1 billion). The absence of a competitive bidding process (there were no other bidders for this project) and the widespread allegations of cronyism created such outrage that the construction project was canceled.

Through the same PPS model, Grupo Higa was granted a contract by Rafael Moreno Valle, a governor of Puebla from the PAN Party, for the construction of the International Museum of the Baroque, with a budget of 12 billion pesos (US$647 million). Another project, still embroiled in controversy, is the aqueduct from Monterrey, Nuevo León, through the Pánuco River that flows into the Gulf of Mexico, to Tamaulipas and Veracruz. This project, originally budgeted at 55 billion pesos (US$3 billion), has yet to be canceled because the new governor of Nuevo León accepted Peña Nieto and Videgaray's undesirable plan. As others have remarked, only collusion between the federal government and its contractors could explain such a high price tag. This comes as little surprise, as

22   CEO of Pemex.

it is the federal government, not the state, that will foot the bill. One more brazen act of cronyism in service to Higa was the contract to expand the hangar housing José María Morelos y Pavón, the presidential airplane. The job, which was budgeted at 1 billion pesos (US$53.9 billion), was not tendered for, as per legal convention, but instead awarded to a contractor without any bidding process.

Peña Nieto has close ties to Hinojosa. It's a matter of public record that the businessman rented planes and helicopters to the State of Mexico, and now does so for the presidential staff. When he was governor, Peña Nieto made frequent weekend trips to Miami using the most luxurious planes in the fleet. It was against this backdrop that Peña Nieto's wife, Angélica Rivera, purchased from Hinojosa what is now known as the White House,[23] a mansion in Mexico City valued at 120 million pesos (US$6 million). Many believe that these transactions are simply *moches,* or bribes. The release of the Panama Papers revealed that Hinojosa has hoarded US$100 million in offshore bank accounts.

Peña Nieto's other favorite business is the Spanish company OHL. Until recently, the director of Mexico's branch, also under Gerardo Ruiz Esparza's patronage, was José Andrés de Oteyza, who was secretary of state for national heritage under President José López Portillo. Another politician with close ties to Salinas, Emilio Lozoya Austin, ex-director of Pemex, also sat on the board of directors of OHL. As with his investments in Higa, once Peña Nieto became governor of Mexico, OHL received public funding to build highways and transport networks. At present, the vast majority of these roads are owned by OHL, and traveling on them costs more than in any other part of the country. Businesses such as OHL thrive in Mexico's climate of cronyism. Audio recordings exist in which OHL representatives can be heard bribing elected officials for publicly funded construction projects. Following Peña Nieto's ascendancy to the presidency, OHL spread its tentacles far and wide, winning contracts all across Mexico, from trains and highway

---

23 No relation to the US White House—it was so named due to its gleaming marble walls.

networks to the construction of power plants for the Federal Electricity Commission (CFE). Their *modus operandi* consists in receiving treasury subsidies and, simultaneously, a commission for subsequent use of the facilities. One example is the multilevel Mexico-Puebla highway, a stretch of road fourteen kilometers long between the Volkswagen plant and the Cuauhtémoc football stadium. The government disbursed 5 billion pesos (US$269 million) for construction and OHL ostensibly put up another 5 billion, at a cost of 650 million pesos (US$35 million) per kilometer. The true cost was less than half of that; and in reality the Spanish firm hardly put up a penny, yet still were granted the right to charge a toll for use of the road for the next twenty-five years.

The same lack of transparency characterized the construction of the new airport in the Valley of Mexico, a pharaonic, costly endeavor riddled with structural flaws. While it is true that Mexico City's Benito Juárez airport has insufficient capacity and required expansion, this could have been achieved, as we proposed, at the military air base of Santa Lucía. Whereas the new airport, Peña Nieto's latest caprice, would require the closing of Benito Juárez and Santa Lucía due to airspace interference. We're talking about billions and billions of pesos going down the drain. Terminal Two of the capital city airport was barely constructed in 2007, and the presidential hangar was expanded. If we add to the cost of these projects and the loss of the closing of the Santa Lucía airfield, we're talking about a staggering waste that would mean huge profits for property speculators, but no social utility whatsoever, to say nothing of the grave environmental costs. Instead of spending 180 billion pesos (US$9.7 billion) on the construction of this new airport, our alternate proposal is to invest 65 billion (US$3.5 billion) in two additional air strips in Santa Lucía. This alternative plan would save the country over 100 billion pesos (US$5.3 billion). Within our proposed budget we could expand Santa Lucía to accommodate international and cargo flights, designate Benito Juárez for flights within Mexico, and create a direct route between the two terminals.

Building the new airport in Lake Texcoco also carries risks of subsidence, as the region rests on a layer of compacted mud. The solid ground lies some fifty meters below the surface. It is possible, as Dutch technicians and business magnate Carlos Slim's company have proposed, that the danger can be reduced by installing a floating platform that would mitigate the risks. However, the proposed costs would be extortionately high. There is no reason, after all, to insist on pursuing the current plan, save for the apparent necessity of brokering morally dubious contracts.

¡Oye, Trump! Speech 4

Without Migrants There Is No Progress

Chicago, Illinois, February 20, 2017

A few days ago, in Los Angeles, I asserted that Donald Trump's campaign against Mexicans and migrants around the world was rooted more in ideology than in economics.

I argued that upon winning the presidency through hateful rhetoric and discriminatory policies, Trump planned to employ the same strategy to remain in power. But a mere month into his term, it is painfully clear that the neo-fascist strategy of blaming foreigners for America's misfortunes is a profound failure. Why? First, because the task of stigmatizing the Mexican people, as Hitler stigmatized the Jews, is legally, morally, and politically indefensible. It is a failure, too, because its chief premise is flawed: it is simply false to claim that American workers lack decent jobs and salaries because of migrants and America's trade relationship with Mexico. During the electoral campaign, Donald Trump and his advisors sowed fear by stating that under current trade arrangements the US automotive industry would move to Mexico, abandoning American autoworkers to penury. Once he secured the presidency, Trump declared that he would impose a tax of 30 percent on Mexican automotive exports. This is sheer demagoguery: if Trump pursues protectionist policies of this kind, the American people will be badly affected. Consumers will be the first in line to suffer but so, too, will many of the businessmen who funded Trump's campaign. The US and Mexican auto industries are highly integrated: while it's true that 70 percent of vehicles assembled in Mexico are exported to the US market, 40 percent of the materials for those cars are built here in the US. Therefore the success of the automotive industry in this country depends, in large part, on its integration with ours. Without the parts and vehicles manufactured in Mexico, it would be very difficult for the US industry to compete with European and Asian competitors. Perhaps the most illustrative example is in car parts, where Mexico occupies sixth place as a global manufacturer. Mexican exports of auto parts constitute 28 percent of the American market. Mexico is one of the main producers of seat belts, seats, airbags, motors, gears, friction wheels, and other parts that are used in the American automotive industry. These components are incorporated directly into the production lines of vehicles in the US. Therefore the final cost of vehicles assembled here in the US is greatly subsidized by Mexican industry. Without Mexican production, the American automotive industry would not be competitive.

The most important components of Mexican industry are the youth, dexterity, innovation, and strong work ethic of the Mexican people. The participation of workers in these productive processes is no less important than that of the companies which employ them. While Mexican labor is first rate, it is also the worst paid in all of North America. In the automotive sector, a Mexican laborer earns US$3.50 per hour, whereas an American earns $34 per hour—that is to say, ten times more. New legislation that increases tariffs or implements barriers on importation of Mexican vehicles and auto parts would only hurt the US and Mexican economies. Furthermore, the effects of these measures would negatively affect even members of the Trump administration.

One such member is Wilbur Ross, Donald Trump's secretary of commerce. According to an investigation by *El Universal*, Ross is the founder and main shareholder of eight auto parts factories in Mexico that provide equipment to the main car companies in the US. Ross's plants in Mexico receive financial subsidies from our government; and they export seats, doors, airbags, panels, consoles, floors, electrical and acoustic systems, among other components for Ford, GM, Chrysler, and other car brands.

In spite of Trump's threats, and given the likely impact on the US economy, we do not expect any significant moves toward protectionism on the part of the US government. And even if our nation were targeted by protectionist measures, we would have recourse to the World Trade Organization. More important than focusing on the empty threat of revising NAFTA, we must work to inform the American people that they are being manipulated into ascribing the failings of the American economy to migrants, particularly those of Mexican origin. It's essential to combat the crusade of hate launched against foreigners by Trump and his advisors.

Those who spread hate and fear will soon be unmasked. We must reach out to lower- and middle-class American workers, explaining that their problems are rooted in the poor distribution of income in the United States and that, compounding this problem, political power is in the hands of businessmen notorious for paying as little tax as possible. We must raise awareness among workers who have not yet recovered from the 2008 economic recession and who, owing to their precarious and hopeless situation, have been brainwashed by this campaign of anti-immigrant hatred. It is essential to appeal to the good hearts of ordinary people, to make them see that our task is to build, here on earth, the kingdom of justice and fellowship for all. A world without walls, poverty, fear, discrimination, or racism. Confronted with Trump's orders to persecute migrants, we must join together to denounce his human rights violations, remembering that the US is committed to respecting the Universal Declaration of Human Rights. As Article 1 states: "All human beings are born free and equal in dignity and rights. They are endowed with reason and conscience and should act toward one another in a spirit of brotherhood." Here in Chicago, as we did in Los Angeles, we express our complete solidarity with our countrymen who have come to the US to make a living and are committed to the economic and cultural growth of this country. We share the same support for migrants worldwide. We must not forget the history of workers' struggles here in this city, in the US, and around the world. One hundred thirty years ago, eight laborers, mostly migrants, were unjustly tried for peacefully demanding the right to an eight-hour day. Five were sentenced to death. Contemporary historians have shown that they were innocent of the crimes of which they were accused, and that the trials were a farce. These historians also revealed that the executions were pursued to intimidate those who might fight for their legitimate rights, and that the executions created a climate of fear not too dissimilar from that which the Trump administration has sought to stoke against migrants today. Jose Martí's words on the Haymarket Martyrs ring true for migrants today: "These are not abominable felons, thirsting for chaos, blood, and violence, but men who sought peace, hearts full of tenderness, loved by those who knew them and who saw the strength and glory of their lives." It is this same sentiment which emboldens us to defend the hardworking migrants of today. On behalf of many Mexicans, we tell you that you are not alone. In spite of these difficult times, know that no one and nothing can stop the triumph of justice and fellowship.

Trump is no match for the kindness of the American people. He cannot destroy hope.

He is no match against justice and the human spirit. He cannot win against the strength of reason and public opinion.

Long live the Haymarket Martyrs! Long live migrants!

Long live the people of Mexico! Long live Mexico!

CHAPTER 4

KILLING THE GOOSE THAT LAYS THE GOLDEN EGG

We have already alluded to several scandals, but perhaps the most outrageous is the corruption that pervades the energy sector in Mexico. The possibilities for corruptly appropriating public assets was the central motivation behind the privatization of the petroleum and electric power industries. One could argue that corruption has always existed in this sphere, but now corrupt officials risk killing the goose that lays the golden egg.

Jesús Silva Herzog, a Mexican economist (and later politician), noted angrily that when the petroleum company El Águila was expropriated, the British owners charged more than the company was worth because Mexican officials "were too generous." In August of 1947, the state agreed to pay a sum of US$81,250,000 for the expropriation, including interest dating back to March 18, 1938. The circumstances around the agreement were shrouded in secrecy; negotiations between Vincent Charles Illing, the British representative, and Antonio J. Bermúdez, director of Pemex, took place at the latter's home over the course of ten days.

Before long, someone, either within the petroleum sector, or from the Mexican government itself, couldn't resist the temptation to make a buck and leaked information to the British press. The leak caused El Águila's stocks to skyrocket, and it was later revealed that senior officials had been in on the leak, and had purchased shares at rock bottom prices.

Profiteering from insider information was nothing new then and remains just as prevalent today. Let us consider a few cases: in May of 1881, during the *Porfiriato's* earliest days, one of the antecedents to contemporary cronyism took shape. Secretary of Finance Francisco de Landero y Coss sold 36,000 government-owned Mexican Railway shares to some close associates. The train line ran between Mexico and Veracruz, and was at the time the only railway in the country. Congress approved the sale after the fact, contrary to a law that required that all transactions of this nature be subject to a public bidding process. Yet, the most significant "irregularity" in the process was the government's decision to sell these shares at twelve pounds sterling per share, when that same day they had been trading at sixteen pounds and rising. Among the buyers was Ramón Guzmán, who six months later acted as witness for Carmelita Romero Rubio in her marriage to Porfirio.

Francisco Bulnes[24] notes that in 1908, when the government bought up shares of foreign companies to create Ferrocarriles Nacionales de Mexico,[25] the treasury secretary's brother, Julio Limantour, took advantage of insider information and, with a credit line at the national bank, bought advance shares through the New York market. These shares were then "sold at a higher price to the Mexican government, represented by the brother of this fervent speculator." Business arrangements of this sort continued throughout the *Porfiriato*; they didn't disappear in post-revolution administrations, and they have been the hallmark of the processes of privatization of banks and public enterprises under *Neoporfirismo*.

At Pemex, the state-owned petroleum company, corruption was relatively restrained from its expropriation in 1938 up until the 1970s. There were companies in the energy sector with ties to politicians, particularly in the area of oil exploration, but throughout production, refining, petrochemistry, and transport, little was contracted out—curbing much of the potential for bribery. This

---

24 A journalist and politician who was known as an influential liberal intellectual figure under the *Porfiriato*.

25 National Railways of Mexico.

doesn't mean that Pemex was free of corruption; in those times, its very logo was a *charrito*,[26] who, people joke, was left bow-legged under the weight of corruption.

The poor management of Pemex worsened during President José López Portrillo's administration, when his friend, the engineer Jorge Díaz Serrano, director of this public enterprise, relied on cronyism to appropriate large quantities of petroleum that had been originally destined for export, taking advantage of the fact that the cost per barrel was skyrocketing. This scandal was so brazenly outrageous that when the price of crude oil collapsed, the once-powerful functionary became the fall guy and was sent to prison on charges of corruption.

Even against this background, the scale of modern-day corruption in the energy sector is unparalleled. From Salinas onward, Pemex and the Federal Electricity Commission have been ransacked like no other companies on earth. Cronyism in the energy sector has resulted in multi-million-dollar losses. We could discuss corruption across all sectors of the Mexican economy, because it's ubiquitous (in the purchase of new and refurbished equipment, services, construction of plants, etc.), but it's more illustrative to provide a brief look at the most lucrative sectors: gas and electricity.

The case of the petroleum industry is an embarrassment. No new refineries have been built since 1979. The last built was in Salina Cruz, Oaxaca; the other five are in Minatitlán, Veracruz; Ciudad Madero, Tamaulipas; Salamanca, Guanajuato; Tula, Hidalgo; and Cadereyta, Nuevo León. The decision to sell crude petroleum abroad instead of processing it here is distinctive of the neoliberal age. Even during López Portillo's rule, despite designating much of our petroleum for export, our refineries still supplied the internal market and hardly imported gasoline. But since Miguel de la Madrid's presidency in 1982, the lack of refinery capacity, alongside the growth in internal demand, has forced the country

26   Diminutive term for a Mexican cowboy.

to import 635,000 barrels of gasoline per day, 60 percent of our national consumption.

In Mexico, we face the unfortunate paradox of being one of the world's major petroleum producers, but also importing more gasoline and petroleum than most other countries worldwide. Gasoline in Mexico costs 30 percent more than in the United States, and often more than in Guatemala, despite that country's petroleum shortage. The abhorrent politics of petroleum in the neoliberal age can be summed up with this statistic: from January to August of 2016 the export of crude oil from Mexico rose to US$9 billion; meanwhile, the imports of petroleum, natural gas, and petrochemicals reached $12 billion. That is to say, there was a deficit of $2.5 billion.

The irrationality of exporting crude oil and importing gas is akin to exporting oranges and importing orange juice. It is sometimes argued that it's cheaper to import gasoline than to refine it in Mexico. This assertion is baseless and absurd. Producing one liter of gasoline requires two liters of crude oil, and while the crude sells at 8.96 pesos,[27] gasoline goes for 13.98 pesos—which is to say, the added value after refining is 35 percent and entails other economic benefits such as the creation of jobs and non-reliance on outside suppliers.

The spokespeople for these so-called businessmen parrot the line that refining gasoline is not profitable; they maintain that, in any case, instead of building new refineries they can just buy facilities that have been shut down or are underutilized in the United States. Yet while Mexico has 6 refineries, the United States has 141.[28] Our neighbors process 19 million barrels of crude petroleum each day, at a productivity level of 97 percent.[29] Mexico's plants can process 1.2 million daily barrels and operate at only 40 percent of capacity. This is rooted in the inability of these refineries to process heavy crude oil, the inefficiency of exporting light crude oil, and in widespread corruption.

27 As of September 2016.
28 http:www.eia.gov/tools/faqs/faq.cfm?id=29&t=6
29 http://www.eia.gov/petroleum/refinerycapacity/table1.pdf

In 2008, bowing to pressure from our movement, Felipe Calderón announced his decision to build a new refinery. Boasting about the jobs it would create, Calderón invited state governments to compete to see which would provide the best site. Ultimately Tula, Hidalgo was chosen. However, as we predicted, Calderón's term ended without even the perimeter being demarcated, and when Peña Nieto took over the project was dropped outright.

Our existing facilities, too, have been allowed to deteriorate. This is not a new pattern; it happened to our petrochemical plants, which were practically abandoned and reduced to scrap. This was not for want of money, as a great deal was earmarked toward maintenance of the facilities. It again comes down to corruption. In 1997, when it was time to reconfigure the Cadereyta refinery, the South Korean firm Sunkyong Limited (SK), the German firm Siemens, and the Mexican firm ICA were selected for the job. The work was supposed to be finished by July 2000, but it took more than double the estimated time. The work was shoddy, and the payout was far more than agreed upon. In November 2001 the auditors found losses of over US$1 billion. Pemex, which had waived national jurisdiction, was sued by the consortium in international courts. Lacking a strong defense, it was obliged to pay an additional $630 million. To this day, no official has been held responsible for the loss of $1.63 billion.

For repairs at the Minatitlán refinery, a contract was granted in 2003 to the Spanish firm La Dragados. However, by 2012, four out of five construction schemes were not yet completed, and Pemex requested additional funds from the treasury for the administrative closure of the project. A job that should have taken four years ran for ten, running over US$2 billion over budget. And no one was held accountable.

The reconfiguration and modernization of the Francisco I. Madero refinery in Tamaulipas was put up for auction in 1999 and the auction process was completed in 2002. At a cost of nearly $2.6 billion, the job was awarded to Pempro, a conglomerate of the Mexican firm Tribasa and Siemens—despite their poor performance with the reconfiguration of Cadereyta. Pempro was awarded these contracts under questionable circumstances and brought in nearly 4,000 laborers and technicians from South Korea, the Philippines, and Thailand, the vast majority without the approval of the National Institute of Migration (INM), leaving local laborers without work. The reconfiguration of three refineries cost over US$7 billion, just to have them running at 40 percent capacity. This is fraud on a staggering scale.

On March 8, 2016, Pemex director José Antonio González Anaya stated that he'd "take advantage of the tools of the Energy Reform" to allow for private sector participation in the reconfiguration of the three remaining refineries (state property in the hands of Pemex): the Antonio Dovalí Jaime Refinery, in Salina Cruz; the Antonio M. Amor Refinery, in Salamanca, and the Miguel Hidalgo Refinery, in Tula. These so-called "strategic alliances" are really just a mechanism for enabling privatization, as was used in the handover of the petrochemicals plant Pajaritos to the Salinista banker Antonio del Valle. Valle invested over $200 million, became a majority shareholder, and then fired 1,500 of the 2,200 employees who worked in the plants. This left maintenance and security in shambles, and led to an explosion at the plant that claimed the lives of thirty-two people.

Though Mexico's corrupt politicians will say otherwise, oil refining remains a viable business. In 2006 there were 680 refineries worldwide, and over the last decade 14 more have been built. In 2008, India began operations at the largest refinery on the planet, with the capacity to process 1,240,000 barrels per day. The complex stretches across 415 acres in a city built expressly for the purpose of housing 2,500 employees and their families on the northwestern coast of Guyarat. The owners, previously in the textile industry, invested $6 billion in the refinery. Construction began in December 2005, and three years later operations began. This demonstrates that it's possible to operate refineries efficiently and without corruption.

Those who maintain that the refinery business is not profitable are either wrong or simply lying. We have access to crude oil, a growing internal market, and the technical expertise to undertake the refining process. It's true that the profit margin is small (and will never compare with the profit margins from *extracting* petroleum since, among other reasons, nature doesn't charge rent); but investment in refinery capacity means creating jobs, saving on transport, and achieving greater economic self-sufficiency. Investment in the refining business is not only profitable, but also strategically smart. One thinks back to Rockefeller, who once said, "The best business in the world is a well-run oil company. The second best business in the world is a badly run oil company."

In truth, the decision not to build refineries was rooted in the desire of Pemex International to maintain its profits from import. Pemex's $25 billion-per-year deals were always shrouded in secrecy. The National Institute for Transparency, Access to Information, and Personal Data Protection (INAI), an organization with a massive budget and well-paid officials, was ostensibly created to combat corruption, but in truth it's been more committed to covering it up. The INAI has never said a critical word about the management of Pemex International, and no one outside their inner circle knows at what price they purchase gasoline in the United States, how much of a cut they take, or even who produces and transports the stuff.

This of course is all in the past: following the implementation of the so-called Energy Reforms, the procedure for buying gasoline and diesel was changed, although corruption is rife. In April 2016, Peña Nieto's government began granting concessions to smaller foreign companies to import and sell gasoline in Mexico. It handed over to the private sector what was once administered by Pemex. In 2015, the Mexican enterprise made 44 percent of its income on the sale of those energy sources, including crude oil exports. This was the sort of cut that powerful officials were taking.

Up to June 17, 2016, sixty-nine permits for gas import totaling around 1,335,000 daily barrels were granted, and ninety-nine permits for diesel import, totaling 1,015,000 daily barrels. This quantity greatly exceeds internal demand; in 2015, Pemex sold 793,000 barrels of gasoline and 385,000 barrels of diesel per day, taking in 355.3 billion pesos (US$19 billion) and 162.2 billion pesos (US$8.7 billion) for each, respectively. This means, on the one hand, that imports could displace national production of these energy sources, and, on the other hand, that this select group of businessmen and shareholders is left with a business worth 518 billion pesos (US$27.9 billion)—3.7 percent of the GDP—and with a net utility of almost 70 billion pesos (US$3.7 billion).

To put this level of corruption in context, consider this: in its request for the extradition of Joaquín Guzmán Loera,[30] the United States claimed that he smuggled seventy tons of cocaine in a single month, with a "street value" of US$700 million. If we extrapolate to a year, then, we're talking about an $8.4 billion business, nearly three times less than the business of importing and selling gasoline in Mexico.

The greatest beneficiaries of these permits are the three companies who manage over 60 percent of authorized imports: the multinationals Gulf Oil and Trafigura-Puma Energy, and the Mexican Grupo Comborsa. They all have histories of influence peddling, ecological catastrophes, and the paying of bribes to win contracts and gain control over the country's natural resources.

Following the advent of NAFTA, the Mexican government set aside quality control standards for gasoline in order to remain competitive and to keep prices low. Consequently, quality declined drastically. This is especially concerning with regards to the health effects associated with high sulphur content in gasoline; we are gambling with the health of the Mexican people in the pursuit of easy money.

Ultimately, the sale of gasoline and diesel fuel is a very profitable business. The government's energy reforms pose an existential threat to Mexico's energy sovereignty. Without public pressure, there will be no incentive to build new plants or to maintain our national refineries. This must be addressed in the 2018 election through a referendum to determine whether to remain on this path or to change it.

*

30   The notorious Mexican drug lord, also known as "El Chapo" Guzmán.

The natural gas situation is very similar to that of gasoline. Until recently Mexico was self-sufficient in natural gas, but since 1993, we have stopped investing in exploration and extraction and instead opted to increase our imports. Meanwhile, the construction of private power plants has multiplied, adding significantly to the demand for natural gas. The business of buying and selling natural gas has had corrupt politicians and influence peddlers chomping at the bit. The contracts in the field are notorious. It should surprise no one that Mexico is the oil-producing state most responsible for burning off gas into the atmosphere.

This excessive burning off of gas originated under Zedillo's government, when the then director of Pemex, Adrián Lajous, made the controversial decision to build a nitrogen plant in Atasta, Campeche, to augment the extraction of crude oil. Production increased for four years, but the nitrogen contaminated the oil and gas wells. Consequently, they were forced to close down over eighty wells, losing around 400,000 daily barrels of petroleum, and burnt off 750 million cubic feet of gas into the atmosphere every day. Though there was an easy solution—gas separation plants require neither a large investment nor overly sophisticated technology—it was not pursued, because those in the upper management of the energy sector are interested solely in personal gain.

Mario Gabriel Budebo, deputy secretary of hydrocarbon energy, commented that "considering the price of natural gas in 2009 of US\$3.61 per thousand cubic feet, the economic value of hydrocarbon gas burned this year is estimated to be around \$921 million. This volume represents approximately 18.5 million tons of CO_2, with grave implications for the environment."[31] Similarly, a Pemex report delivered to the Mexican Stock Exchange stated: "During the third quarter of 2015, emissions increased by 509 million cubic feet daily, largely due to the incident that took place at the Abkatún A-Permanent platform, as well as delays in attempted landfill gas captures." This represents, at an average cost this year

31 *El Universal,* May 9, 2010.

of $2.70 per thousand cubic feet, $1.37 million daily, or over $500 million annually. Worse still than this massive waste of money is the environmental damage incurred as a result of burning off natural gas.

Neoliberals didn't resolve the financial and environmental problems of gas burn off in the Cantarell (one of the largest oil fields in the world); instead, they kept buying more gas from foreign companies. Calderón himself celebrated a contract with the Spanish energy company Repsol for the provision of 500 million cubic feet imported from Peru. Much like Peña Nieto's predilection for the foreign firm OHL, Calderón favored Repsol. Recall that the first contract for multiple services granted to a foreign firm—in direct violation of the Constitution—was during Felipe Calderón's time as secretary of energy and president of the board of Pemex. On November 14, 2003, without other companies being allowed to bid for the job, Repsol was granted a contract for $2.4 billion to develop the oil fields of Cuenca de Burgos, Tamaulipas.

The appendix of the contract, entitled "Catalog of Maximum Prices," spells out its outrageous terms: the infrastructure was acquired at 120 percent of cost; and as for maintenance, 320 percent of direct cost was paid. What's more, the price per unit was unchanged regardless of whether the firm used new or used materials. Moreover, the contractor was allowed to conduct its own inspection processes and approval and certification of all materials. Even more outrageously, the hidden costs of tariffs and taxes were not factored in until after the contract was awarded.

While foreign firms made windfall profits, our country picked up the tab. For these onerous contracts doled out to Repsol, Tecpetrol, Petrobas, Teikoku, Schlumberger, and Halliburton, among others, Pemex has paid out over $5 billion, with the pretext that gas production would increase by 50 percent in the Burgos Basin—yielding 500 million cubic feet daily. However, five years later production has only increased by 63 million cubic feet, just 4 percent of the promised increase. During this same period, Pemex increased production at its non-contracted fields from 1 billion to 1.3 billion cubic feet, or 35 percent. In short, these contracts did little for the company and, given the grossly inflated price, the contracts represented a huge attack on the public interest.

Mexico's leading auditing institution, the Auditoría Superior de la Federación, denounced Pemex (during Calderón's tenure as president of the board of Pemex when he was secretary of energy) for selling Repsol bonds at artificially low prices. This practice was justified in two ways: first, it was claimed that the price of shares was going to decrease, and that funds were needed to finance Pemex. Recall that in October of that same year, Repsol had been granted a contract worth $2.4 billion to produce gas in the Burgos Basin—which, of course, raised its stock value. As to the need for finance, Pemex never offered the auditors any proof whatsoever that selling the shares was the best course of action. Regardless, in order to sell those shares, Pemex issued a bond expiring in 2011, convertible to stocks, and situated it in the tax haven of Luxembourg. Months after the sale, the shares grew in value, leading Pemex to register losses of $655 million.

In 2005, the Federal Electricity Commission (CFE) was exploring a project for the provision of natural gas and the construction of a regasification plant in Manzanillo, Colima. With zero regard for transparency, Repsol was made aware of these projects and, with this privileged information, obtained the right to extract gas from the region of Camisea in Peru in December 2005, knowing that they could sell it in Mexico and the eastern United States. Yet at the time, Repsol had no legal right to supply natural gas in our country. This raises an obvious question: How did Repsol know, in 2005, that it could sell gas to the Commission, a year and a half before the project was even announced?

The Federal Electricity Commission did not release a call for bids until June 6, 2006. When they did so they stated that the contract would be for a period of twenty-five years. It was also stipulated that a bid clarification meeting would take place in September 2006. When the new administration took the reins, Repsol negotiated directly with Felipe Calderón, and, disdainful of established legal procedures, hammered out a deal from the offices of Juan Camilo Mouriño, then secretary of the Office of the President. On

September 18, 2007, the CFE awarded a contract to Repsol for the provision of 500 million cubic feet of natural gas per day, without allowing counter-offers from alternative bidders. The contract was estimated at being worth some $15 billion.

Corruption grew even more entrenched under Salinas. On September 22, 1992, Congress approved a reform that allowed foreign firms to receive contracts to install energy generation plants. This was a violation of Article 27 of the Constitution, which states: "It is the Nation's exclusive right to generate, conduct, transform, distribute, and supply electrical energy whose purpose is the provision of a public service. In this sense, no concessions will be granted to private individuals and the Nation will make use of all goods and natural resources required for these ends."

Nevertheless, from Salinas onward, offshore companies— largely based in Spain—began their creeping expansion into Mexico's energy market. Public sector plants were shut down or run below capacity, effectively opening the market for transnational corporations. This was backed up by a vicious propaganda campaign that asserted the energy sector needed to modernize, or Mexico would face calamity. These maneuvers opened the door to characters such as José Córdoba Montoya and Claudio X. González, two of Salinas's advisors, who held stocks and other interests in the companies.

Alfredo Elías Ayub, who served as director of the Federal Electricity Commission, was another person who benefitted significantly. Previously the deputy minister of mining under Salinas, he oversaw the privatization of mining companies like Cananea and presided over the division of 9,456,722 acres of mineral reserves among three syndicates: Alberto Baillères's Peñoles, Jorge and Germán Larrea's Grupo Mexico, and Carlos Slim's Grupo Carso.

Under the direction of Elías Ayub, the Federal Electricity Commission became a "world class" business specializing in overcharging energy to Mexican consumers and subsidizing foreign firms. Today, the CFE buys nearly 50 percent of the energy consumed in this country at extremely elevated prices: in 2016 it earmarked nearly 60 billion pesos (US$3.2 billion) for this purpose. Concurrently, public sector energy plants were either left to rust or were underutilized. But the decline of Mexico's industrial infrastructure does not concern the well-paid business executives and defenders of neoliberal dogma. Two years ago it was discovered that a group of Mexican politicians were keeping huge amounts of money in Switzerland.

This laundry list of corruption demonstrates that the recent waves of privatization are rooted in the perverse ambition of the same group of people that has cannibalized our national assets. The decision to privatize was not taken because of technical, financial, or administrative considerations; this decision was taken purely in order to facilitate corruption and fraud.

Emblematic of this practice was the granting of the first block of territory opened for petroleum exploration in shallow waters, to Sierra Oil and Gas, a subsidiary of Black Rock Funds. Barely a year before, the company had been purchased by Jerónimo Marcos Gerard Rivero, Salinas's brother-in-law. Subsequent rounds favored ex-government functionaries who sat at the helm of private petroleum corporations.

Even as petroleum prices fall, these so-called businessmen still profit. For example, in 2012 the cost of extracting one barrel of crude petroleum was around $10, with around $5 designated to go toward bribes, but it was sold at $94, and the public finance system took in a significant portion. Now it goes for $40; however, private enterprise gets $25 and the nation receives only $15. Another approach is to reduce profits on paper by artificially inflating production costs, as Repsol, Schlumberger, Halliburton, and others have done. Ultimately, it is a great deal for private firms—and a terrible one for our country.

These crooked politicians, blinded by their lust for money, have gambled with our nation's future. Neoliberal politicians ended nearly one hundred years of energy sovereignty. They did not heed general Cárdenas's warning: "The government or individual who hands over natural resources to foreign entities betrays the nation." I will finish with the words of Adolfo López Mateos,[32] who wrote a note on September 27, 1960, when he nationalized the electric industry, in which he wisely professed:

To the people of Mexico: I put electric energy back in your hands, as it belongs solely to the nation, but do not trust that in later years some with malicious intent will not attempt to return it to the hands of foreign investors.

"Not one step back" was the motto of Lázaro Cárdenas del Río upon nationalizing our petroleum. Today, electric energy has its day. People of Mexico, I absolve you from any loyalty to a future government that might hand over our resources to foreign interests. It is clear that Mexico must modernize our technology and invest resources effectively to achieve energy independence; it would be absurd to affirm otherwise. However, outside investment is not a requirement. Only a traitor hands over his country to foreign nationals; we Mexicans can manage our affairs better than any country can do on our behalf.

When a foreign State asks me if they can enter our energy industry, I respond that we're just barely achieving the independence from foreign invasion from which we freed ourselves not so long ago.

We Mexicans are happy to invest in American petroleum or in the production of electric energy, if they want a foreign investor. However, Mexico's Constitution makes it clear: our energy resources are the sole and exclusive property of the Mexican people. Arguments to the contrary are a betrayal to the nation.

Industrialization does not require giving up our resources to the highest bidder, nor the indiscriminate handover of our country's legacy.

The corruption of the energy industry will be a contentious matter of debate in the campaign cycle of 2018. The Mexican people must choose not only the next president, but also the political economy we want moving forward. I hope that the people will decide to re-establish the autonomy of our natural resources, including petroleum and electricity, in service to the *pueblo* and to the nation.

---

32   President of Mexico from 1958 to 1964.

¡Oye, Trump! Speech 5

Our Development Project

El Paso, Texas, March 6, 2017

It is my great pleasure to be in El Paso, Texas, one of the most charming of American cities. Some hundred meters from here, on the other side of the river, president Benito Juárez and his cabinet took refuge for about a year to continue the fight in defense of our national sovereignty. Later, another Mexican hero, Francisco Madero, a preacher of democracy, led from that same border town, Benemérito, the revolutionaries who defeated the *Porfirista* dictatorship.

El Paso, Texas, is one of the oldest cities in the US. Founded during the Spanish colonial period, it was then part of Mexico and, when Texas gained its independence, it was annexed to the American Union. Here, in El Paso and across the border in Ciudad Juárez, is where our two nations are most intertwined. The Mexicans and Americans along this border region are irrevocably linked by history, culture, work, commerce, and friendship.

This shared history contradicts the efforts of American politicians to foster division through their hateful and nationalist propaganda campaign. It's true that this fear mongering secured Donald Trump the presidency, but it won't allow him to maintain his grip on power forever.

There is no doubt that in Texas, as in other parts of the US, there exist pockets of racism and conservatism; but that same border zone is rife with shared customs and relationships between Mexicans, migrants, Anglo-Saxons, African Americans, and all other varieties of people who inhabit this area.

However, there is growing evidence that racism has penetrated the minds of many Americans. Testimonies abound of how, in recent times, mistreatment and xenophobia abound in cities across Texas and New Mexico.

Therefore, our most important task is addressing the American people: we must reach out to those who have been brainwashed into believing that foreigners—particularly Mexicans—are the cause of their problems.

We must shout from the rooftops that America First is folly; first must be, in any place on earth, justice and universal fellowship.

We must explain with well-reasoned arguments that the economic ills that workers face are not a result of migrants or the people of Mexico, but are due to bad governance, unfair privileges, and poor distribution of income. Problems that blight both this nation as well as our own. We must reach out to those who have fallen for Trump's lies. Let them see that it is immoral and absurd to persecute the Mexican people and that mutual respect and cooperation will help our respective nations better than tension and hate.

We can't discount the possibility of convincing Trump of the error of his foreign policy; particularly regarding his derogatory attitude toward the Mexican people and our nation.

We are committed to our development program. By supporting growth, job creation, and well-being, we can address the root causes that drive migration, instability, and violence. We repeat: walls and force won't fix social ills; only successful and sustainable development and promotion of well-being will do that.

The most humane and effective approach for reducing migration is to provide assistance to our rural areas, supporting the productive sector, creating jobs and improving the salaries of Mexican workers. Sooner or later we will reach that goal because, regardless of what the US government decides with respect to its foreign policy toward Mexico, we will soon eradicate corruption in Mexico. This will allow us to free up resources to improve the living and working conditions in our nation.

The new democratic government will always be respectful toward the US government, but we will assert our sovereign rights. For example, we will unconditionally defend the right of our people to make an honest living wherever they choose. Under our administration, the Mexican consulates in the US will dedicate themselves full-time to defending our countrymen.

We will establish a bilateral relationship with the US based on cooperation that aids development. We will defend migrants but,

concurrently, pursue economic policies that generate jobs and provide Mexican people with work and dignity in their places of origin, where their families, customs, and culture reside.

We will promote the regional development of Mexico,
from South to North, with the goal of allowing the people to
remain in their *pueblos*, by increasing opportunities for work
and well-being.

For example, we will plant 1 million hectares of timber and fruit
trees in the southeast; we will expand tourism in the Caribbean and
Mayan and Olmeca archeological zones; we will build two large
refineries on the Gulf of Mexico in order to reduce gas imports and
lower the price of energy; we will create an economic and commercial corridor in the Isthmus of Tehuantepec; we will expand the
ports of Salina Cruz and Coatzacoalcos; we will create a train line
for shipping containers, taking advantage of our strategic position
between the Pacific and Atlantic oceans.

Across the country we will guarantee prices for crops in
order help to stem migration and achieve food self-sufficiency.
In tandem with this initiative, we will help the construction
industry to create jobs, by investing in public works (streets, hospitals, schools, housing, and the introduction of new services)
and re-activate the economy from below, beginning with the
pueblos of Mexico.

We seek balanced economic growth across the country—not
just in relatively affluent pockets, as has been the case for the past
thirty years. We will support development across the Mexican side
of the border with the United States.

Along the 3,185-kilometer border with the US, we will create a
duty-free zone to promote investment, technological development,
and the creation of jobs.

This will help us to retain workers in our territory. Across the
span of the border, on a strip of land at least twenty kilometers
wide, we will subsidize productive activity, reducing the price of
energy sources and electric energy and increasing salaries.

Let me explain why we will pursue these policies. Prior to the
US invasion of 1848, which resulted in the loss of half our territory,

a Tamaulipas governor, Ramón Guerra, released a decree in 1858 authorizing the first zone of free commerce in that state of the Republic. Then, in 1884, during the *Porfiriato*, President Manuel González extended the duty-free zone from Matamoros to Tijuana, passing through Coahuila, Chihuahua, Sonora, and our then territory in Baja California. The duty-free zone extended from the US border twenty kilometers into Mexico. From 1888 commerce grew and Ciudad Juárez was born. Later, during the post-revolutionary period, in 1933, President Abelardo Rodríguez instituted a similar zone, which was endorsed in the case of Baja California and Sonora by all future presidents until, in 1993, president Salinas de Gortari ordered a suspension of fiscal support for the zone. Needless to say, the zone prospered while it had the necessary support. The crisis of violence seen at the border and across our nation today can be attributed to the failure of the neoliberal economic model that abolished vital government aid to the countryside, producing poverty and forced migration. Neoliberalism forced the Mexican people to leave their homes.

In light of this history, we will re-establish the duty-free zone along the US border. Our plan entails the following:

1. Pushing customs zones south from twenty to one hundred kilometers south of the US border.
2. In duty-free zones, income tax will be reduced by 20 percent.
3. Value added tax will be about 8 percent on average, half of what is currently charged. Specifically, in Mexico's border towns we will apply the same tax rate as in the US. More specifically, a tax rate of 8.5 percent will apply on our border with California; that rate will be 8.2 percent on our border with Arizona; 7.5 percent on our border with New Mexico; and 8.2 percent on our border with Texas.
4. We will reduce excise taxes in order to establish tariffs and prices comparable to the US in gasoline, diesel, and electric energy.
5. Throughout this duty-free zone we will at least double the minimum wage. Justice demands it. There is no risk

of inflation because, as previously stated, we will reduce VAT taxes and energy costs. The aim is to gradually standardize the salaries between that region of Mexico and the US. Recall that an automotive assembly laborer on the Mexican side currently earns $3.5–4 per hour, while an American earns $34/hour—eight to ten times more.

6. Across the duty-free zone we will pursue an urban development plan including the regulation of land use, the introduction of water and drainage systems, the paving of streets, housing, the construction of nurseries, sports facilities, cultural spaces, schools, hospitals, and other public works.

We will pursue this plan in 2018, alongside the broad transformation of Mexico. Until then we will continue to engage with the American public regarding Trump's irrational campaign against Mexico, centering on the protection of migrants facing persecution by the US administration.

I want to remind you that migrants are not the only victims in this region. On the southern bank of the Río Bravo lives a population devastated by crime caused both by bad economic policy and absurd security strategies employed by the state to combat the very problem they created. In recent years, we've seen a policing problem escalate into a full-fledged "war" that has claimed thousands of lives without achieving anything at all. The numbers are tragic: in ten years, from 2007–16, there have been 208,000 murders and over 1 million victims of violence.

The final years of the Salinato[33] unleashed, in Ciudad Juárez, the horror of femicide, which today extends to a good part of the country. Hundreds of women have been murdered not far from here with fierce cruelty, amid the indolence and corruption of municipal, state, and federal authorities. No one has been held

---

33 A reference to the term of Carlos Salinas de Gortari, fifty-third president of Mexico.

accountable for the vast majority of these deaths, and officials don't even bother identifying the bodies.

Women, migrants, citizens, and young people deprived of their place in the world must not remain victims of blind violence caused, in large part, by an economic policy which, along this border more than anywhere else, deserves to be described as criminal.

A little over a year ago, not far from here, Pope Francis said:

One of the greatest evils our youth face is the lack of educational or work opportunities that allow them to escape poverty and isolation. Faced with no real options, many resort to drug trafficking, repeating the cycle of violence.

They are brothers and sisters who have been expelled by poverty and violence, by drug trafficking and organized crime. Faced with these circumstances, they are trapped, with no escape. They not only suffer poverty, but these other forms of violence. It is injustice which radicalizes the youth; youth who are then persecuted and threatened when they try to escape the cycle of violence and the hell of drug use. And how many women have had their lives unfairly taken!

But, addressing labor unions and businessmen, he offered words of hope:

There is always the possibility of change. There is still time to react, to transform, to modify, and to change that which is destroying us as a people, that which is degrading our humanity.

We continue to fight for a better society. We will rebuild our country, defend the dignity of our people and we will, above all, transform Mexico to eradicate the destitution that either drives away or destroys its citizens. We can end the anxiety and pain that afflicts our border regions, turning those parts of our country into a prosperous and peaceful place to live. The future of Mexico is in our hands.

I invite you to join me so that we may begin to develop our homeland from the Río Bravo in the north to the Usumacinta, making ours a free, just, and democratic nation, without corruption or violence. A new state, without hate, enlightened and fraternal.

CHAPTER 5
WHITE COLLAR CRIME

The corrupt spoils of the neoliberal era are brazenly on display. Salinas's beneficiaries, who previously were not on the map, now appear on lists of the world's richest men. Salinas must have done alright for himself as well, though it's hard to be precise about this. Even though neoliberals detest the comparison, Salinas is like the old dictator, Porfirio, who kept his assets shrouded in great secrecy. Equally shrouded in mystery are the reasons why Salinas conceded Telmex to Carlos Slim instead of Roberto Hernández (whom he later appeased through the handover of the National Bank of Mexico).

Meanwhile, it's widely known that Carlos's brother, Raúl Salinas, made a fortune from private individuals who benefited from the privatization of banks and public companies. Some time later, Raúl threatened to expose the details of his brother's bank accounts in Switzerland. In October 2000, when Salinas intended to return to Mexico with a book extolling his time in government, Televisa aired audio of phone calls between his siblings Adriana and Raúl, in which the latter threatened to implicate Carlos in the acts of corruption for which he, Raul, was serving time. A 1998 report by the Government Accountability Office (GAO) titled "Raúl Salinas, Citibank, and Money Laundering Allegations" states that from 1992–94 the ex-president's brother transferred $100 million "through Citibank Mexico and Citibank New York to private banking investment accounts in Citibank London and Citibank Switzerland." This was done through front men, and the money came from five Mexican banks: Bancomer, Somex, Banca Cremi, Banorte and the Bank of Mexico. These accounts were opened under false names and, thereafter, Raúl Salinas maintained in his defense that this money was "loaned" by bankers and businessmen with ties to the family.

Another person who benefitted was Pedro Aspe, who served as secretary of finance under Salinas and was in charge of determining, alongside Raúl, those who were to receive funds from the public purse. Aspe has been, among other things, president of the board of Televisa, and is the primary shareholder of the airline Volaris. He owns the companies Protego, Intellego and Diavaz Offshore, among others. He is also a professor at ITAM (Mexican Autonomous Institute of Technology), which has installed countless technocrats in power during the neoliberal period. Among its students have been at least three recent treasury secretaries. For an insight into the institute's academic orientation, one need look no farther than at the disastrous state of the national economy. Beyond their dishonesty, the intellectuals at ITAM are technocrats who view themselves as *Científicos*.[34]

Ex-president Ernesto Zedillo is another example of the mindset. Despite his antipathy toward Carlos Salinas, who accused him of being a traitor, Zedillo imposed the same neoliberal politics of pillage as his predecessor. He, too, has embraced that school of thought, much like Pedro Aspe, Guillermo Ortiz, Francisco Gil Díaz, Jaime Serra Puche and others; an ideology that has festered in American universities and which dictates that the State has no need to meet its social obligations, and should not stop the transfer of public resources to private hands. For them, the State is a burden, except when it serves their interests, as was the case in the bailing out of financial institutions during the financial crash. According to that logic, money allotted for the poor is derided as *populism* or *paternalism*; yet the moment it's earmarked for those at the top it is

34 Technocratic advisors to Porfirio Díaz who advocated for modernization.

labelled *development*. During Salinas's rule, when Zedillo served as secretary of public education, he pushed for a reform of Article 3 of the Constitution that would roll back the right of children to a free education. From then on, as a result, the State stopped investing in middle school and advanced education. Soon thereafter, middle and high schools were unable to accommodate the vast numbers of qualified students who wanted to attend, and excluded millions of students from poor families who were unable to pay for schooling.

This technocratic plan of Zedillo's was made manifest in his response to the economic crisis of December 1994. The flight of capital out of Mexico that resulted from the government-ordered devaluation of the Mexican peso led the economy to contract by 6.2 percent, a disaster the likes of which hadn't been seen since 1932. In this instance, the government's first move and priority was to bail out businessmen and bankers with public funds, without a second thought as to the economic hardship faced by the vast majority of the Mexican people. The technocrats rushed to pin the blame on each other; the Zedillistas said that when they took over the state the economy was hanging by a thread, and the Salinistas shot back that while that might be true, it was the Zedillistas who broke the string. What is certain is that the bailout targeted the largest and most influential borrowers. Toward this end, in 1996, at the beginning of Zedillo's term, the federal government created the Coordinating Unit for the Bank-Entrepreneur Agreement (UCABE). The UCABE was created to restructure debts for large companies, costing the treasury millions. The program was sold on the premise that once the rich were doing well, the resulting wealth would trickle down.

Later on, the Banking Fund for the Protection of Savings (FOBAPROA) came into being. It transferred private debt to the public, in direct violation of the Constitution, as only Congress is legally empowered to authorize public spending. But these officials bought high-risk portfolios and offered promissory notes "with the full support of the federal government, in service to the banks." This "bailout" was an altogether terrible deal for the state; indeed, it received no shares in exchange, unlike the bailout in the

United States under Barack Obama. Soon thereafter, the crisis of December 1994[35] paled against the massive debt that FOBAPROA had assumed. In his second state of the union address, Zedillo assured the people that the bailout would cost no more than an additional 180 billion pesos (US$9.7 billion). Three years later, that number had grown to 850 billion pesos (US$45.8 billion). From 1995 onward, the state has paid out 600 billion pesos ($32.3 billion) in interest payments alone, trapping the treasury under a mountain of debt. According to the Institute for the Protection of Bank Savings (IPAB), successor to FOBAPROA, by December 31, 2009, the net liabilities doled out by the institution had reached 816 billion pesos (US$44.2 billion). And according to their September 2016 report, the net debt of the IPAB had reached 855 billion pesos (US$46.1 billion), 4.46 percent of the GDP. The treasury technocrats have estimated that the debt will take at least seventy years to pay off.

To highlight this shameless plundering of public funds by the bankers, a look at a few key dates proves illustrative. In 1999, Citibank, which then owned Banca Confía, received 6.4 billion pesos (US$345 million) from the federal expenditures budget; Banco Santander, 5.5 billion (US$296 million); Promex, 5.1 billion (US$275 million); Banorte, 4.3 billion (US$231 million); and Bilbao Vizcaya, 4 billion (US$215.8 million). Our institutes of higher education did not fare as well. UNAM received 7.5 billion pesos (US$404.6 million); IPN, 3.5 billion (US$188.8 million); UAM, 1.3 billion (US$70 million); and the National Pedagogic University, 245 million pesos (US$13.2 million). While the bankers had their bonanza in 1999, health spending for the vast majority of Mexicans was miserly. The General Hospital received 772 million pesos (US$41.6 million); Juarez Hospital, 245 million (US$13.2 million); the Institute of Cardiology, 258 million (US$14.7 million); the Institute of Nutrition, 320 million (US$17.4 million); the Institute of Pediatrics, 338 million

---

35 The Mexican peso crisis stemmed from the swift devaluation of the peso against the US dollar, leading to a spike in inflation and a severe recession.

(US$18.4 million); the Children's Hospital, 331 million (US$18 million); and the Psychiatric Institute, 73 million (US$3.9 million). The nation's anti-poverty campaign, then known as Progresa, received 8 billion pesos (US$436.2 million), while concurrently, the bailout of Banca Serafin cost 77 billion pesos (US$4.1 billion)—nearly ten times the sum. One bank alone received more funds than the entire budget of states like Tlaxcala, Nayarit, Zacatecas, Aguascalientes, Colima, Campeche, Yucatán, Quintana Roo, Querétaro, and Baja California Sur, among others.

Despite this, Ernesto Zedillo, the main architect behind the creation of this black hole of public finances, enjoys not only complete impunity, but the reputation of having been a good leader. Of course, this praise comes largely from the wealthy elites who did well under his rule. Beyond money, Zedillo also sought to win the trust of domestic and international financiers, and to ensure himself a career at the end of his term. As president, he bailed out the bankers, and upon completion of his term he joined the board of Citigroup. Similarly, after handing over Mexico's public railway infrastructure to four conglomerates[36] he was appointed as an advisor to the board of Union Pacific Railroad which, along with Grupo México, brought Mexico's 150-year-long operation of passenger trains to an end.

This *modus operandi* has been rampant in the neoliberal age. Adrián Lajous, director of Pemex during Zedillo's presidency, is now an advisor to the multinational Schlumberger. This petroleum company has been a perpetual darling of the neoliberal state. Between February and August 2013 alone it received contracts amounting to 7.6 billion pesos (US$414 million), many of which were awarded to companies without going through a bidding process. Other directors of Pemex under the administrations of Zedillo, Fox, and Calderón are now employees or shareholders of private petroleum companies.[37]

---

36 Kansas City Southern of México, Union Pacific Railroad, Transportación Marítima Mexicana, and Grupo México.

37 Carlos Ruiz Sacristán is the general director of Sempra Energy México; Ramírez Corzo, Juan José Suárez Coppel, and Gonzalo Gil White (son of Francisco Gil Díaz, ex-treasury secretary), are shareholders of Oro Negro, while Jesus Reyes

Guillermo Ortiz was deputy finance minister under Salinas, secretary of finance under Zedillo, director of the Bank of Mexico and president of the board of Banorte, the very bank he later privatized and bailed out with public funds. Francisco Gil Díaz, treasury secretary under Fox, is another person who has been accused of dishonesty and corruption. This career bureaucrat got his start when banker Roberto Hernández recommended him for the position of treasury secretary. Gil had been deputy finance minister during Salinas's term and thereafter became director of Avantel, a telecommunications giant owned by Roberto Hernández. Not surprisingly, the Fox administration's first big deal was the sale of Banamex to Citigroup. The bank— of which Roberto Hernández was the primary shareholder—was sold for $12 billion, without paying a cent in taxes. Similarly, Bancomer was sold for $10 billion to the Spanish multinational Bilbao Vizcaya Bank. In the neoliberal age, Mexican banks and corporations are sold off tax free, which would never be accepted anywhere else on Earth. Proponents of neoliberal doctrine are quick to extol the virtues of rule of law, globalization, free commerce, and competition—as long as they're exempt.

The foreign firms and governments who have participated in these acts of theft are not constrained by even the mildest norms of international ethics. Spanish firms and officials have been shameless in their lobbying and bribery of Mexico's political elites. When Gil Díaz served as treasury secretary, the state built 21,000 kilometers of fiber optic network for the state electric industry, at a cost of 30 billion pesos (US$1.6 billion); after his stint in public service when he joined the Spanish telecommunications group Telefónica, it received a concession to use the

---

Heroles González Garza is on the board of OHL and associate of Raúl Livas Elizondo (ex-director of Pemex Petroquímica), at EnergeA. Carlos Morales Gil, who alongside Felipe Calderón was director of Pemex Exploration and Production, is now the manager of the petroleum corporation PetroBal, recently incorporated by Alberto Baillères, the second richest man in Mexico.

network for twenty years for the pittance of 850 million pesos (US$46.3 million).

*

The case of Vicente Fox is a particular embarrassment to our country. He is hollow and unprincipled, much like Calderón and Peña Nieto, but even cruder and more brutish. Fox has never been much of a businessman. He was a manager at Coca-Cola; ultimately, a hireling for the rich. He embraced this role fully in his time as president. He stands accused of failing to act as large donors evaded taxes through the practice of fiscal consolidation, wherein firms hide earnings and fabricate losses.

Unsurprisingly, the group of businessmen who funded Fox's presidential campaign were richly rewarded to the tune of 12 billion pesos (US$654.4 million) in value added tax (VAT). In 2001, influential lawyer Diego Fernández de Cevallos, a proud PRI supporter and Salinista who became the legal representative of Jugos Del Valle,[38] received 1.4 billion pesos (US$76.3 million) in tax refunds. This arbitration, carried out before a court decision could be reached, required that these funds come from cuts in state budgets. Corruption is so legitimized by the government that the Federal Institute for Access to Public Information (IFAI) kept secret the names of those companies who gained millions from Fox's tax programs for a period of twelve years.

Gastón Azcárraga, who supported Fox throughout his 2000 campaign, was compensated with ownership of Mexicana de Aviación,[39] much as Calderón "sold" Aeroméxico[40] to his supporter José Luis Barraza and others who upheld his electoral victory. Barranza has since come forward as an "independent" candidate in the state of Chihuahua. In short, the PAN has used Mexico's

---

38 One of the largest Mexican beverage producers.

39 Mexico's largest airline until it ceased operations in 2010.

40 Mexico City-based airline.

public sector airline to pay for political favors, and, in the case of Mexicana, allowed it to be liquidated.

The Fox phenomenon was a product of its time: people were sick of the PRI and wanted something different. On the left, we were unable to present a coherent policy platform. We didn't promote our Alternative Nation Plan, and the fight between PRI and PAN became polarized. This became a vote simply to remove PRI from power, and thus voters succumbed to "lesser-evilism." In the end, things changed only to stay the same. Fox's arrival merely strengthened the old regime. Fox is a traitor to democracy. His worst offense was imposing Calderón upon the electorate through electoral fraud. How different things could have been if the will of the people had been enacted in 2006.

I met with Fox in September 2000. He had invited me to lunch in Las Lomas, at a house that was lent to him by Roberto Hernández, owner of Banamex and a supporter of his campaign. During the same period, Fox vacationed at Hernández's second home in Punta Pájaros, in the Mexican Caribbean.

Fox suggested that we should fight for tax reform together. He planned to expand VAT to food and medicine, and asked for my support. I turned him down outright, explaining that this so-called reform would hurt the poor and middle class and allow the rich to continue to profit at the expense of ordinary Mexicans. I suggested that he take a closer look instead at financial speculators, who make huge sums that go wholly untaxed. I mentioned to Fox the case of Roberto Hernández—without realizing I was sitting in his home.

"They do pay taxes," he protested. Yes, the poor might pay more up front, but the gains of the wealthy, he stated, would "trickle down." Needless to say, we did not reach an agreement. But it's important to note that even before assuming the presidency, Fox brought with him the blueprints to advance broad neoliberal structural reform, including privatization of the electric and petroleum industries, rolling back of worker protections, and other plans proffered by technocrats to serve a small and corrupt class of elites.

Although I could go on describing Fox's many misdeeds, I'll give just one more example of his misrule. As president, Fox expanded his ranch, buying up nearly 1,500 acres, installing an irrigation system, a new hacienda, and even an artificial lake. Satellite photos tell the whole story and provide damning evidence of this; if our institutions were just, he would be tried for embezzling public funds.

*

Of Mexico's long line of politicians who pandered to the elites, Felipe Calderón Hinojosa towers above all others. He is the prototypical conservative, a PAN member through and through. He is deeply rooted in right wing ideology and takes inspiration from the reactionaries of Mexico's past. Until recently he took part in public tributes to Agustín de Iturbide, who established a monarchy following the national independence movement, although he was forced to abdicate the throne not long after. Needless to say, Calderón does not hold in high esteem the legacies of Juárez and Cardenas. He's spoken publicly of his esteem for Spanish dictator Francisco Franco. Even more tellingly, he has remained a stalwart of the party that has perpetuated the same economic program since 1983, and whose most tireless proponent has been Carlos Salinas de Gortari. In his time as chairman of the PAN, he engineered the great FOBAPROA scandal alongside Zedillo. Recently, the Spanish multinational Iberdrola, which dominates energy sales to the Federal Electricity Committee and received lucrative contracts under Calderón's reign, named him a member of the board. Bertolt Brecht's words ring as true as ever: the worst of all thieves are "the corrupt officials, the lackeys of exploitative multinational corporations."

Felipe Calderón summed it up in one word: hypocrisy. In the interest of transparency, I'll admit that I'm not sympathetic to conservative thought. Someday I'll elaborate on this, but for now suffice it to say that I find conservative ideology hypocritical. Calderón has simply embraced his own hypocrisy. He is the quintessential embodiment of right-wing hypocrisy; of those who wax eloquent about purity but are motivated solely by vulgar ambition; who go to church or temple but forget the Commandments; who confess their sins as a matter of routine each Sunday just to get a blank slate to sin again throughout the week.

In Tabasco, we say *ish careca,* something like "gross" or "ugh," and this is an expression close to the PAN aristocracy's heart. To them, everything is *ish careca*—ordinary people are trashy, classless, stupid or immoral. They only hide their racist and classist sentiments when it serves their ambition. They'll loudly condemn Moreira, Mario Marín, Romero Deschamps, Beltrones, Elba Esther,[41] and even Peña Nieto, but their silence is deafening when one exposes their pacts with these characters, to say nothing of Salinas,[42] Yunes Linares,[43] and other miscreants.

Many writers and journalists are sympathetic to this conservative mentality. In 2006, so-called democrats either kept silent or were outright complicit in electoral fraud, some even signing an open letter asking that the electoral results be respected instead of pursuing a widely demanded recount. PAN is quick to decry the corruption of PRI while turning a blind eye to their own. They decry Peña Nieto, with good reason, given the extravagance of the White House (the extravagant mansion purportedly bought by Peña Nieto's wife), but they ignore Calderón's purchase of a

41 Humberto Moreira, former governor of Coahuila charged with money laundering and embezzlement and prosecuted for ties to the notorious Zetas gang; Mario Plutarco Marín Torres, former governor of Puebla who was caught on recording agreeing to jail journalist Lydia Cacho after accusing a wealthy textile magnate of pedophilia; Carlos Romero Deschamps, Pemex union leader widely accused of corruption and fraud; Manlio Fabio Beltrones, former president of the Senate accused of using his influence to protect drug lord Amado Carrillo Fuentes; and Elba Esther Gordillo, who served as leader of the National Education Workers Union, the largest labor union in Latin America, before being arrested for fraud and embezzlement.

42 Former president of Mexico whose brother was arrested for illegal enrichment upon allegedly laundering millions of dollars in drug money.

43 Governor of Veracruz accused of illegal enrichment upon allegedly siphoning money from the Institute for Social Security and Services for State Workers.

presidential plane that rivaled or surpassed Obama's, despite the massive budget of our neighbor to the north. They are scandalized by the Duartes in Veracruz and Chihuahua[44] but applaud Yunes Linares and Cabeza de Vaca.[45] The prevailing mentality seems to be that they are good-for-nothings but they're *our* good-for-nothings; indeed, one rarely hears Fox or Calderón questioned over corruption. Perhaps they did not notice that during Calderón's tenure as director of Banobras,[46] he granted himself a home loan, and once caught, transferred the loan to the commercial bank Inverlat. Calderón, too, steadily bought up his neighbors' land and was left with an enormous residence.

In the 2006 presidential debate, I alleged that Hildebrando Zavala, Calderón's brother-in-law, took in over 600 million pesos (US$32.7 million) in government contracts during Fox's term. I also claimed that he received contracts from Pemex and the Federal Electricity Commission when Calderón was secretary of energy and, what's more, made this fortune completely untaxed. Calderón denied these facts, and his brother-in-law promptly sued me. The suit was quietly withdrawn, and the media maintained a complicit silence. When Calderón was president, Zavala sold 77 percent of his company shares to Carlos Slim. Juan Ignacio Zavala, another brother-in-law of Calderón's, was contracted as a communications advisor to the Spanish firm Prisa, which publishes the daily newspaper *El País*. Although in most regards the PRI and PAN are one and the same, one point of differentiation is that PRI officials are corrupt egotists, whereas PAN officials are corrupt hypocrites.

Calderón himself is a good example of the latter. On October 28, 1998, I participated in a debate moderated by journalist José

---

44 Javier Duarte de Ochoa, former governor of Veracruz. As evidence of corruption and links to organized crime emerged, he became a fugitive before being caught and extradited to Mexico by Guatemalan officials. César Duarte Jáquez, former governor of Chihuahua, currently facing an investigation for corruption.

45 Francisco Javier García Cabeza de Vaca, governor of Tamaulipas with alleged links to the Gulf Cartel.

46 National Bank for Public Works and Services of Mexico.

Gutiérrez Vivó, wherein Calderón asserted that PAN would not approve FOBAPROA.[47]

AMLO: You agreed to resolve the FOBAPROA issue without accountability for those responsible, and not in the presence of any auditors.
GV: OK, he's going to answer.
FCH: We are not going to approve FOBAPROA, Andrés Manuel . . .
AMLO: What I'm concerned with is the following: Are you going to approve the judgement on FOBAPROA alongside the PRI, yes or no?
FCH: No!
GV: He said he wasn't going to.
AMLO: Got it.
FCH: OK.

A month and a half later, at dawn on December 12, with 325 votes in favor from the PAN and PRI, FOBAPROA was approved. Subsequently, Calderón handed over our motorways to the very businessmen who had been bailed out by FOBAPROA at a cost of 160 billion pesos (US$8.7 billion). Needless to say, those same businessman had donated generously to Calderón's campaign.

When I was head of government, Salinas and his colleagues tried to foment a scandal because I once wore a Tiffany watch. The watch cost 5,000 pesos (US$272) and was gifted to me by César Buenrostro and his wife for Christmas in 2003. *La Crónica*, a paper with ties to Salinas, reported that it was valued at 80,000 pesos ($4,000). I clarified the real price, at which point Calderón made an opportunistic show of buying it off me. He even mailed me a check as a publicity stunt.

Calderón demonstrated a total lack of ethics during the presidential campaign. Following the election, I wrote to him calling for

47 Mexico's government-run Bank Insurance Fund that assumed private bank debt with public funds.

a recount. I closed my note thus: "If the tribunal will not implement a recount, and instead asserts your victory outright, the integrity of the vote will be forever in question and questions of election fraud will not be resolved. To millions of Mexicans, you will be a spurious president, and our country deserves better than to be led by someone lacking moral or political authority."

But an immoral man is incapable of acting with dignity. During the campaign, journalist Denise Maerker asked Calderón: "Did you agree to such a negative campaign, one so steeped in attacks against your opponent, because you thought it was the only way to catch up to AMLO's lead?" He answered: "The negative campaign was led by the PAN." "Were you OK with that?" she asked. Felipe laughed and said: "Yes. At the end of the day, it got results."

There is a mountain of evidence that demonstrates that Calderón did not win the election. At one point, now governor of Coahuila Rubén Moreira approached the podium of the Chamber of Deputies and asserted: "Calderón stole the presidency." It was a heated session, culminating in PRI legislators chanting "Spu-ri-ous! Spu-ri-ous!" Without hesitation or shame, the then chairman of the PAN, Manuel Espino, confessed (as if it were an accomplishment) that this was indeed the case, that the election was stolen; Fox and many others have seconded this claim. It is my hope that professor Elba Esther Gordillo and Joaquín Guzmán Loera, aka El Chapo, will testify in support of the claim of electoral fraud and thereby support our democracy.

Last year, during the campaign to elect the governor of Zacatecas, Calderón accused David Monreal[48] of having links to the Zetas. These unsubstantiated accusations are right out of his playbook: he did the same in Veracruz, pitching Yunes Linares over our candidate. The bishop of Zacatecas addressed these practices in a homily one Sunday: "The candidate who runs a dirty campaign will run a dirty government." The relevance to Calderón was stark: he defrauded his way into the presidency and turned our great nation into a laughing stock. Calderón, in a desperate bid for

---

48 Zacatecas senator.

legitimacy, waged a war against organized crime that led to innumerable deaths. Calderón's brilliant plan simply served to stir the hornet's nest.

Some bull-headed conservatives still maintain that Calderón was a good leader. But, much like Fox, he was an utter calamity for Mexico. In 2000, the PAN came to power presiding over the highest petroleum prices in world history. Fox managed petroleum income to the tune of $335 billion, and in windfall profits alone made $10 billion per year between 2004 and 2006. Similarly, in 2017, Calderón's *de facto* government received $12 billion in surpluses due to high petroleum export prices, and in 2008, $16.5 billion. That year, the Chamber of Deputies set a price per barrel of $49, but it was sold at $84.30 per barrel on average. From 1901, when we first began utilizing this natural resource, to the present, no president of the republic has ever presided over such enormous revenue gains from oil. Between 2007 and 2012, Calderón oversaw "extra" income due to high petroleum prices to the tune of $100 billion.

These funds were used to subsidize the expenses of their associates. They were squandered to maintain the status of high public functionaries. The state did nothing to reduce this massive bureaucratic waste. On the contrary, in 2007 the budget was raised by 154 billion pesos (US$8.3 billion). In 2008, it added 190 billion pesos (US$10.3 billion) more, and in 2009, another 150 billion pesos (US$8.1 billion). That is to say, in three years our expenditures grew by nearly 500 billion pesos (US$27.2 billion). During this administration, this massive bureaucratic waste ballooned from 1.2 trillion pesos (US$65.4 billion) to 1.8 trillion pesos (US$98.1 billion), while economic growth in that same period was a paltry 13 percent, four times less. Under Calderón, public debt went from 1.7 to 5.2 billion pesos (US$92.7 million to US$263.6 million); that is to say, it grew by 207 percent. Ineptitude, corruption, and waste were the causative factors driving this mess.

The murky case of Oceanografía and its majority shareholder, Amado Yáñez Osuna, perhaps best illustrates this widespread corruption. This company, with close ties to corrupt upper management at Pemex, was granted contracts that were staggeringly lucrative. Their period of greatest growth tracks perfectly with twelve years of PAN governance. Throughout this period, Oceanografía "won" roughly 160 contracts that brought in nearly $3 billion. Their downfall came about when, in 2014, Banamex accused the company of falsifying invoices and fraud. Amado Yáñez Osuna now sits in jail, and one of his associates is a fugitive. How is it that, despite their ties to Mexico's elites, they were still ultimately held accountable to the law? The answer is simple: Banamex had more powerful connections still. Oceanografía picked the wrong clients: those up top don't let themselves be swindled so easily.

Yáñez had a penchant for luxury: he indulged in private planes, soccer teams, yachts, luxury vehicles, parties in Miami, and other extravagances. According to those close to him, his weakness is high-end watches. The luxury brand Audemars Piguet lists him as a distinguished buyer in a 2012 pamphlet.

Yáñez Osuna had a special edition watch made with the name of his company engraved. He ordered a hundred, specially designed for him, with their logo and corporate colors to celebrate the fortieth anniversary of Oceanografía. One can only imagine what it must have cost for a luxury watchmaker—whose watches regularly figure in the millions of dollars—to take on this bespoke project. Needless to say, these watches were not intended for sale, but as gifts to clients, friends, and politicians.

This is a telling example of how lobbyists amass huge fortunes in a short period of time. These vermin generate not only inequality, but deep resentment among the people. It's terribly unjust that while millions of Mexicans struggle in poverty, a select few live in opulence. We are not against those who earn a comfortable living through hard work and talent; honest businessmen deserve our respect and protection. But real businessmen are not wasteful; they are austere, for they know the true value of money. The problem is that this crisis of ill-begotten wealth is the product of shady and illegal means, and that it is squandered on offensive displays of wealth. During Peña Nieto's term, the economy has grown by a paltry 2 percent annually, while, according to Bain and Company, the growth in luxury consumer goods in Mexico grew by 12 percent. According to Luxury Society,[49] members of Mexico's elite each spend approximately US$313,000 per year on average on luxury goods. One final statistic, this time from *Knight Frank Global Cities Survey*, revealed that Mexico City sits at 32nd place among the 40 best cities for the wealthy to shop—above Berlin, Washington, D.C., Boston, Cabo, Auckland, Buenos Aires, Río de Janeiro, and Tel Aviv. May we never forget that corruption begets poverty, frustration, hate, violence, social decomposition, and inequality. For the good of all, Mexico must return to honesty.

49   A content aggregator for industry executives.

REBIRTH
¡Oye, Trump! Speech 6
The Wall of Death

Phoenix, Arizona, March 7, 2017

The desert that extends toward the south of this city is an immense graveyard. Thousands and thousands of Mexicans and Latin Americans have been left to die of hunger, thirst, or exposure. Miguel Méndez, born here, in Arizona, to Mexican parents, migrants from Sonora, spoke of the border thus:

There goes the procession
Marching over a field of bones
To the beat of derogatory chants
The earth swallows itself
What kind of world is this, which buries its children at dawn?

Poet and novelist Miguel Méndez was an exemplary man. At age fourteen he earned a living in these lands as a builder and day laborer. He ended up as a professor emeritus at the University of Arizona and left us a body of work that represents an enormous contribution to Chicano, Mexican, and American literature. He died in Tucson a few years back, and I find it important to begin this address by taking a moment to honor his memory.

The desert is naturally arid, but it is human cruelty that makes it deadly. Ever since Bill Clinton authorized the construction of fences to seal off old border paths around Tijuana and El Paso, migrants have had no choice but to cross a desert full of dangers.

Neither the fences built at the end of the last century nor huge increases in the Border Patrol did anything to halt immigration. They only made it more dangerous.

Migrants continued to risk their lives in the hands of heartless *polleros*[50] and gangs who lurk in the border region. They

---

50 People who smuggle migrants across the border.

also must evade the Border Patrol, and even civil militias who, horrifically, hunt for migrants. If the migrants made it that far, they still had to face a long and unforgiving journey through the desert.

In this part of the world, death stalks migrants just as it does the people attempting to cross the Mediterranean, but the media does not lend us the same attention as the victims of those tragedies. Deaths slowly pile up, unyielding, ever so quietly.

Of course, those who undertake this journey are not following some suicidal impulse: economic necessity pushes them on this perilous track.

Dishonest Mexican officials have lied to us, presenting the economic flight of millions as natural. Rather than creating jobs or providing people with dignified work conditions, education, health, or housing, they have allowed this migration to continue unchecked; the result has been a true humanitarian catastrophe. They no longer question the fact that one of the greatest sources of foreign currency in our country is the remittances those banished workers send to their families.

On this side of the border, one finds the hypocrisy of an economic system hungry for cheap labor that legislates their persecution, that seeks to fortify the border and greatly increase deportations. The truth is that US politicians themselves do not seek to impede the entrance of foreign laborers but regulate it according to their will, depending on the demands of the labor market. In truth, US immigration policy has been a valve that regulates the workforce at the will of US business.

Trump's persecution of migrants is mere electoral demagogy; he has deceived many US citizens with the narrative that Mexicans are stealing their jobs, and now he intends to exploit that lie to extend his time in the White House. But he knows perfectly well that the US economy cannot sustain itself without migrant labor and the very low salaries those migrants receive. To a large degree they sustain America's ability to stay competitive in agriculture, industry, and services worldwide.

The pretense of building a wall follows this hypocritical logic. If it is ultimately built, this wall will not staunch the flow of workers from one country to another; it will simply make things much more dangerous. This is a criminal idea.

History teaches us that no wall will stand forever. Neither the wall of Troy nor the wall of Jerusalem could withstand sackings and attacks; the Great Wall of China could not prevent the Mongol invasion, and the Maginot Line did not prevent the German invasion of France during the Second World War. This wall will do still less, because south of the US exists not an enemy but a country sacked by greedy officials, and by dishonest politicians that have left millions with no recourse but to find a living elsewhere.

As the US southern border faces no real threats against which to defend, Trump's wall will not be defensive. On the contrary, it would function oppressively, like the Berlin Wall, or be exclusionary, like the enormous fence built by Israel to confine the Palestinians. But, above all, it would exist as a propaganda tool to deceive US workers battered by neoliberalism and the fear of criminality. Trump will use this wall to make these people feel that the government is doing something to protect their jobs and secure their safety, while ensuring construction firms can make astronomical profits.

I want to stress that the construction of this wall would impede the free transit of members of indigenous cultures; the yaqui, the pápago and others, original owners of these lands between Sonora and Arizona.

As the great novelist Carlos Fuentes wrote, "When we exclude, we lose. When we include, we win, and we shall never recognize our own humanity without recognizing that of others."

We reject the erection of this monument to hypocrisy and cruelty because we want no more families separated and no more bones in the Arizona desert. We must join forces with the people of this great country that repudiate the persecution of migrants, that stand against oppressive fences and that still treasure the wise words of the great American poet Robert Frost:

Before I built a wall I'd ask to know
What I was walling in or walling out,
And to whom I was like to give offence.

Though we remain in a region dominated by conservatism, we must not stop appealing to the better instincts of the people of Arizona. Human beings are not bad by nature; if they are pushed to reflection and empathy, they will act with compassion and discover their own inner goodness.

All human beings possess a conscience. One must not believe, as oppressors have maintained for generations, that only they, the oppressors, were men of "science and conscience," a claim that was used to uphold infamies like subjugation, exploitation, and slavery.

It's evident that for diverse reasons—poverty, ignorance, manipulation, and others—human beings are often slow to identify the meaning of existence, which transcends our material needs. But it's never too late. It's always possible from one moment to the next for our conscience to awaken and ask: "What is the meaning of life?"

Reflection of this sort brings out the best in every individual. In that moment, we liberate ourselves from the tyranny of our baser instincts, and we begin the process of unlearning the many lies we have been taught.

With these truths we must convince the American people that they are blinded by hate against migrants, that they persecute these people for no reason but racial, class, religious, or cultural prejudice.

We must speak with those who were deceived by Trump until they reflect on the inhumanity of erecting a wall to close off the US and convert it into a spiritual wasteland. We must make them understand that this is an affront to liberty, justice, human rights, and universal fellowship, and a negation of their nation's fundamental values. We must explain, moreover, that this grotesque wall won't fix any of the problems it aims to solve, though it will produce a great deal of suffering. We must recall that peace and tranquility, here and in Mexico, as everywhere else, are not fruits of the use of force, but of justice.

Let's touch the hearts of the American people; let's remind them that true happiness resides not in the accumulation of material goods, titles, or fame, but through spiritual well-being; that is to say, being at peace with ourselves, our conscience, and our neighbors.

CHAPTER 6

RESCUING THE STATE

Mexico will not grow strong if our public institutions remain at the service of wealthy elites. The state has been sequestered by a small minority, and this is the primary cause of our national malaise. We are living in a country that is a republic in name only. Constitutional protections apply only to select groups. The first thing we must do is to democratize the state and retool it as an engine of political, economic, and social growth. We must rid ourselves of the myth that development requires blind acquiescence to market forces. The state cannot escape its duties to the people. It exists to guarantee its citizens a just and dignified life, and to guarantee their safety and well-being. Its basic function is to prevent the few who have much from abusing the many who have little.

Our reclamation of the state must be accomplished through peaceful, legal, and democratic means. We must then consider what will be done with Mexico's political *mafiosi* when our movement prevails. Mexico's central problem is the concentration of power in the hands of a few political elites. Yet, if we are committed to the ideals of democracy, we must dutifully consider our approach.

First, I reassert that not all the rich are evil, that we are not against those who—through hard work and determination—invest money, create jobs, make profits, and are committed to the growth of Mexico. We are against those who amass large fortunes based on fraud and favoritism. We are against ill-begotten wealth, and the political corruption that upholds social and economic inequality. I believe that for Mexico to prosper, we need everyone on board. Unfortunately, what has risen to the fore has been lust for money above all else. This is what we fight against.

During the 2006 campaign, despite the state's vicious propaganda campaign against me, I tried to convince people that we needed real and meaningful change, and that our victory was a threat to no one. I affirmed that businesses would benefit greatly from the revival of public life, because corruption harms us all. But the elites would not listen. Instead they opted for fraud, and stole the election. And so they went on, hidden away behind their gated communities, armored cars, and bodyguards, instead of supporting the revitalization of public life.

Now, I want to say to the powerful elites that despite the harm they have done to our country, we hold no grudge against them. If we are victorious in 2018, there will be no retaliation; we will simply not tolerate any attempts to take advantage of the vulnerable again. We emphatically assert that what we need is justice, not revenge. What we seek is the economic, social, political, and above all, moral revitalization of Mexico. We seek to turn a new page in Mexico's public life, with a president who is not beholden to private interests, but only to the people of Mexico. If we set hate aside, we can advance toward a better society. The line from our hymn to Chiapas will then ring true: "May we forget hateful revenge, may bitterness come to an end, may hope be ours, and also love."

No group, however powerful or important they may be, can continue to conspire against the social good in their own self-interest. Nothing and no one could ever be worth more than the well-being and happiness of the people. The new state will be a staunch defender of freedom, and people will be able to focus on the work they find fulfilling. Of course, we will also have to introduce new norms of legality: we will embrace business, but not corruption or impunity; the treasury will work truly and meaningfully for the people; we will favor the poor; we will protect natural resources; the wealth of the nation and the fruits of our labor will be distributed with justice; and never again will the privileges of the few be upheld by the oppression and suffering of the many.

As for policy: I believe that recent structural reforms have not helped the people, and have, instead, been quite harmful. However, we will not respond to an edict with an edict; we will ask the people if they wish to keep the reforms in place, and we shall enact their will, ensuring everyone a voice in governance.

This doesn't mean that we should be silent: our next leader should be steadfastly committed to the public interest. It is essential, I would maintain, to reclaim our energy sector on behalf of our national development; to administer it efficiently and honestly, to reduce energy prices (thus benefiting the consumer), and to push private industry to create jobs.

Should the majority be opposed to the energy reforms that have been put in place, we will immediately pursue the relevant legal proceedings to reverse them. This goal will be far more feasible if we win not only the presidency, but a majority in Congress. Even so, changing laws and canceling contracts takes time, but it is well worth doing. We must return the energy sector to the people. It cannot persist as the exclusive domain of corrupt politicians, lobbyists, and profiteers.

*

Our foreign policy must be moderate and restrained, without taking a central role in global affairs. Our respect for the principle of nonintervention requires us to be prudent. We know that since 1821 and throughout the nineteenth century, Mexico's most important foreign policy aims were to secure independence and the defense of our sovereignty. Due to foreign intervention, our foreign policy has since focused on the defense of our national interests as, according to liberal norms, the state has every right to govern itself independent of the will of foreign powers.

The foundations have been laid for a Mexican diplomatic strategy built on the principles of nonintervention and respect for sovereignty. Nonetheless, despite notable exceptions like the negotiations in Contadora Island where the US invasion of Nicaragua was prevented, there has been a steady decline in our commitment to these values from the 1980s onward. Indiscriminate adoption of the neoliberal model coupled with a weakened economy has led us to this place. The illegitimate government of Carlos Salinas, faced with unyielding protests following the election, gave rise to a major alignment with US foreign policy. Rather than seek reconciliation through government accountability, they opted for authoritarianism, seeking the support and legitimacy abroad that they could not find at home.

In 1995, facing a financial crisis provoked by technocratic inefficiency and corruption, Zedillo's government offered the US entry to our petroleum sector in exchange for a $20 billion dollar loan. One could argue that there was no alternative, but ultimately, our sovereignty was jeopardized due to the irresponsible management of our internal affairs.

After Vicente Fox's electoral victory, our foreign policy became frivolous and overextended. The so-called "change government" was characterized by a love of the spotlight that distanced us from our constitutional principles and our strong diplomatic tradition. Felipe Calderón and Peña Nieto, to our great chagrin, have subjected our nation to ridicule. Today, Mexico's image abroad no longer commands respect. In the public eye, Mexico is characterized by violence, corruption, and poor governance.

The foreign policy we advocate will be backed by a strong domestic policy, by cautious diplomacy, and an adherence to the principles of self-determination and nonintervention. We seek a pacifist approach, one that favors restraint over force but asserts juridical equality with the United States. We seek international cooperation for mutual development, peace, the defense of human rights, and environmental conservation.

One central focus for us is our southernmost border. We seek to correct the maltreatment suffered by Central American migrants and to uphold their human rights. We will build close friendships and working relationships with Latin American and Caribbean nations, especially regarding Cuba, with which we have historic ties of friendship. Mexico could benefit from closer relationships with Africa, Europe, Asia, and Oceania—and not strictly of an economic nature. Diversifying our foreign policy presents the opportunity to expand trade relations, but beyond that, to seek out a new global order wherein globalization need not entail neoliberal hegemony.

As for the United States, we will build a relationship premised on mutual respect and benefit. For obvious reasons, we should pursue the Good Neighbor policy.[51] Our geographic proximity to the foremost military and economic power on earth, shared investment in migration and security issues, and our historic and cultural ties favor a strategy of dialogue and cooperation.

Lately, this cooperation has been restricted to security issues, with little focus on the underlying causes of violence and migration to the United States. For this reason, we feel that now is the time to propose a radical change in this relationship. Our task ahead is to convince the officials of our neighbor to the north that, for the good of both nations, it's more efficient and humane to practice a politics of cooperation and mutual development rather than to seek, as we currently do, cooperation in the context of the security state.

Economic and social issues will not be resolved through coercive measures. Neither military assistance nor intelligence services nor transfers of helicopters and arms will resolve the violence and conflict that plague our nation. By the same token, the migratory flow will not be stemmed by building walls, conducting raids, deporting people or militarizing the border. The Mexican people who try to earn a living in the United States do so out of necessity, not choice. They risk it all to find work to mitigate their hunger and poverty.

For this reason, the United States must expand, and, above all, redirect its aid to Mexico. We are ready and willing to work toward a new bilateral agreement based on cooperation leading to development and mutual aid. We have not ruled out the possibility of signing a bilateral agreement to reinvigorate the economy and create jobs in Mexico, including economic rehabilitation programs

---

51 Foreign policy position held by Franklin Roosevelt that centered on nonintervention in the affairs of Latin America.

along the border, which will benefit each of us. This, of course, would be based upon respect for the sovereignty of both nations.

To reiterate, our foreign policy must be an extension of our internal politics. If our country is well-run, if there is honesty, justice, development, and political stability through democracy, we will be respected and respectable. History has demonstrated that when foreign powers perceive us as weak and divided, we are more vulnerable to those who would seek to enslave us. In sum, our foreign policy will be prudent, respectful, cooperative, and firm in the defense of our sovereignty.

*

The new administration will defend the right to free speech and political agency. We will work toward a stronger democracy, shaped by the ideals of President Francisco I. Madero. During his term, democracy flourished as never before. Madero had a deep respect for the rule of law and the separation of powers. On June 5, 1912, in response to San Luis Potosi governor Rafael Cepeda, who had asked if he would remove a district judge who wouldn't help with recruitment efforts, he remarked: "I do not wish anyone to be forced to enlist against their will, and those are not grounds for his removal [...] It is my hope that our judges will be independent thinkers; we don't want them to be hostile to the state, especially when they're as patriotic and prudent as you; but neither do we want their unconditional allegiance, lest the judiciary lose its autonomy."[52]

Madero was equally committed to upholding the decisions of Congress and to upholding the freedom of the press. So strong was his conviction that Madero himself faced criticism for not paying off the media, as Porfirio Díaz had done. Without question, Madero's greatest contribution was his sincere respect for democracy. Who else has believed so fervently in our democracy, or

---

52 Alfonso Taracena, *La verdadera revolución Mexicana (1912–1914)* (México: Editorial Porrúa, 2008), 86–87.

worked so tirelessly to realize its ideals? Madero believed sincerely that by establishing a democratic republic, Mexico could address its problems and advance toward liberty, justice, and prosperity. Madero not only left us this great legacy, he also told us how best to achieve it. His words are unwavering. In May of 1911, he addressed a *New York World* journalist:

Upon coming to power, I seek to embody two principles: The first, as sanctioned by the Constitution, and falling upon me to uphold it, is that there must be no re-election.[53] *Another is effective suffrage.*[54] *To accomplish this goal one must reshape electoral law, and this falls to the people. My central responsibility is to facilitate the free expression of the will of the people, in the hopes that the law will be a genuine expression of that will. In short, I pledge to be the friend and defender of the* pueblo's *liberties. At this historic time in Mexico's development, I consider all else secondary.*[55]

Once in power, he demonstrated a principled respect for suffrage. Madero, like no other president since, conducted clean and fair elections. A few examples: On January 16, 1912, he wrote to Manuel M. Alegre, governor of Veracruz, stating that in local elections "it's essential to be upright, but I'm sure you have the vote of the people."[56] Three days later he reminded Alegre that he was "committed at the end of the day to support whoever secures the most votes."[57] "I repeat," he said on January 23, "it's all the same to me whichever candidate wins, as long as he who secures most votes is elected. These are the principles we have fought so hard for."[58]

53 A relic of the dictatorship of Antonio López de Santa Anna, the Mexican constitution asserts that no president may serve a second term.

54 This became a campaign slogan in the anti-Díaz movement.

55 Alfonso Taracena, *Historia extraordinaria de la Revolución Mexicana* (México: Editorial Jus, 1972), 62.

56 Alfonso Taracena, *La verdadera revolución Mexicana*, 11.

57 Ibid., p. 12.

58 Ibid., p. 15.

Finally, on January 29, he expressed his satisfaction, noting, "The results show complete freedom in elections."[59]

On January 25, 1912, Madero wrote to General Jerónimo Treviño, the strongman of Nuevo León politics, "You know that our government rests on fair suffrage through and through, as only a state with the consensus of the people is stable. For that reason, I beg you to address governor General Estrada and other influential people across the state, in hopes that they will uphold the will of the people in this election."[60]

There are countless examples of Madero's support for democratic elections. In Michoacán, the Catholic leader José Elguero raised questions about the election of Miguel Silva, feeling he had gained an advantage through demagoguery, for he preferred to "tell people what they want to hear," while recognizing that in his private life he was kind, honorable, and a loyal friend. As for irregularities in the electoral process, he committed to accepting the Chamber of Deputies' ruling and exhorted all to do the same.[61] On July 28, at a meeting in Pachuca, Hidalgo, an official stated that in his native village of Tulancingo, they had held legitimate elections for the first time. Madero responded that all subsequent elections would be free and impartial.

Madero's impartiality toward *Porfirista* candidates or outright opponents speaks to his integrity. Nemesio García Naranjo, one of Madero's most committed detractors, was elected to the district of Lampazos, Nuevo León without resistance.[62] In Tabasco, "recalcitrant *Porfirista*" Tirso Inurreta's electoral victory was respected, despite Madero being nearly jailed without reason while campaigning.[63] With regards to Madero and Porfírio Díaz, Elguero celebrated "the contrast between a democratic president who learns the names of contenders to political office the same day

59 Ibid., p. 22.
60 Ibid., p. 19.
61 Ibid., p. 109.
62 Ibid., p. 135.
63 Ibid., p. 115.

as the public, and the old establishment that had a list ready to go months before."[64]

For a brief interval in our history, we had free and fair elections under Madero. This was achieved during a time of political turbulence, and without having a longstanding democratic political tradition. This is the legacy of Madero: a president who is sufficiently committed to the cause can ensure democratic elections and a government that represents the will of the people. In that sense, Madero has had no equal. No other president in Mexico's history has contacted his contemporaries in government, pleading that they abstain from vote manipulation and respect the will of the people.

I assert that if our movement succeeds, we will further Madero's legacy. The will of the people will reign supreme. No longer shall treasury money be used to fund bribes and buy loyalty; as the Constitution requires, there will be full freedom of expression, and censorship of the press will not be tolerated. State communications will not be biased; fraud will be outlawed; government functionaries will be empowered to ensure an adherence to the Constitution and our laws, but they'll be subject to those same laws when they try to advance their own interests. In sum, no one and nothing will supersede the sovereign law of our people.

64 José Vasconcelos, *Ulises Criollo*, ed. Claude Fell (México, Conaculta, 2000), 474.

¡Oye, Trump! Speech 7

New York and Liberty

New York City, March 13, 2017

Liberty is one of the values that defines this great city, funded and developed by men and women who fled from oppression and intolerance. The Dutch fled here from religious persecution and armed secessionists. This city gave shelter to African Americans who escaped slavery in the South, to Jews who fled persecution in Europe, and to Italians who saw in this land the hope of a more prosperous life. Here, the great José Martí sought refuge to organize the fight for the freedom of Cuba. And from here he wrote:

Liberty is the definitive religion, and the poetry of liberty the new form of worship. It soothes and beautifies the present, deduces and illuminates the future, and explains the indescribable purpose and seductive goodness of the Universe.

In more recent times, Asians, Latin Americans, and Africans have arrived, seeking to free themselves from the very worst oppression: hunger.

New York's great tradition of liberty was first realized more than a century ago, when the French Republic gifted New York the Statue of Liberty so that, from the horizon, it could greet immigrants from all corners of the globe. This monument was also a gesture of affirmation of republican values in a France still facing reactionary attempts to restore the monarchy and a physical symbol of fellowship between people.

From this exercise of liberty by millions of individuals arose another central value of this city: pluralism and tolerance, peaceful and fertile coexistence between people of distinct ethnicities, ideologies, religions, and colors. On this island, dozens of languages coexist, and this linguistic diversity, far from isolating people, has brought them closer together. The world recognized those fundamental principles by establishing the headquarters of the United Nations here.

Thus, despite the challenges you face, I celebrate the fact that you and hundreds of thousands of Mexicans are living and working in a city that continues to be a sanctuary for liberty and tolerance.

However, we must not forget that you are here by necessity. You, like many others, have been victims of a neoliberal political system that has been imposed on our country for over thirty years, and that has impoverished our people to satisfy the ambition of a small minority who have devoted themselves to pillage and corruption.

In the neoliberal era, migration grew because, during this same period, Mexico's economy was in a state of stagnation; our rural areas were abandoned, jobs weren't created, and hunger and poverty unleashed instability and violence. Migration is the clearest and most painful proof of the exclusionary nature of the neoliberal model.

You are here because instead of remaining in our country or resorting to crime, you journeyed in search of prosperity. Thanks to that, you are helping your families; the remittances you make to your families, totaling over $24 billion per year, sustain, in large part, the economy of Mexico.

In this paradoxical and bitter reality, a mix of heroism and misfortune, you must now confront a new problem: the persecution of migrants with the support of Donald Trump. This is the central reason for our visit. We came to express to you our most profound support and solidarity. We've gone on this tour throughout the Union to defend migrants, Mexican and otherwise, from the campaign of hate promoted by the new US administration.

I've said it elsewhere and I repeat it now: it is villainy for Trump and his advisors to speak of Mexicans as Hitler and the Nazis spoke of Jews, just before launching their vile campaign of persecution and extermination.

We are convinced that this is a demagogic electoral strategy, which may have helped Trump to secure the presidency, but it will not allow him to remain in power, let alone secure his re-election.

Beyond all this, it is absurd to want to close off this great nation to foreigners. The United States was built with the efforts of men and women from all over the world. Without migrants, the US could not compete with Asia or Europe. What's more, thanks to the hard work and talent of those who have come from elsewhere, New York has overtaken London as the global capital of finance and Paris as the hotbed of artistic movements.

Nevertheless, a campaign of hate against Mexicans and foreigners is taking hold amongst American conservatives and must be countered. We must invoke the universal principle of fraternity.

We must make clear to American workers and businessmen that, if they are facing economic challenges, it is not due to migrants; that crises, here and in the rest of the world, result from the unjust distribution of income and wealth.

We must convince and persuade those Americans who were brainwashed by Trump's campaign rhetoric that "America First" is a fallacy; that justice and universal fellowship are more important than national borders.

We must raise awareness among Americans of good faith who have been tricked by the propaganda campaign against Mexicans and foreigners; we must counter the dissemination of hate with accurate information that will help our movement throughout the US.

We have come to New York to file a complaint with the Office of Human Rights at the United Nations against the campaign of hate directed at the Mexican people, against the order issued by Trump to begin construction of a border wall, and against his plans to persecute migrants from a variety of backgrounds.

But the most important reason for our being here at this meeting is to tell you that in Mexico we are fighting to combat corruption and impunity and that, through these efforts, we will achieve the revitalization of our nation.

With a democratic and honest government, you and millions of migrants will be able to freely choose if you want stay here or return home to a country where your work, well-being, and safety will be guaranteed.

Our country and our *pueblo* are struggling, but this crisis is transitory and better days are coming. Mexico has many natural resources and a hard-working people. All we need is a government that is democratic, just, and honest, and I can assure you that is coming soon.

In these times of struggle, amid government repression on both sides of the Río Bravo, I know you are resisting and dedicating yourselves to the betterment of both countries. Let me quote to you what General Ignacio Zaragoza told the Mexican people who set out to defend their country against the French invaders: "We face the best army in the world, but we will win because you are fighting for the homeland."

Let's not lose hope or certainty in a better future. The Mexican people are heirs to a great civilization. We have overcome betrayals and invasions, we've toppled dictatorships and achieved greatness. Very soon we will restore Mexico, and Mexico will be yours again.

CHAPTER 7

HONESTY IS THE WAY OUT

Mexico's last best hope is an honest government. Honesty is a treasure. Fostering it will help us grow. It will allow us to invest in the development of our people and combat the misery unleashed by the "harsh but necessary" measures that have been imposed to benefit an elite few.

Corruption, as we've seen, is the driver of inequality and suffering in our nation. Dishonesty both by governments and by powerful elites has led to a stark deterioration of public life in Mexico; these crooks have tarnished our reputation and blatantly stolen public goods. Nothing has harmed Mexico as much as corruption. For over two decades, according to Transparency International, Mexico has had a constant and systematic corruption problem. This is confirmed by the Corruption Perception Index, where Mexico scored a mere thirty-five points out of 100.[65]

Thanks to the elites, the problem of corruption is not debated or addressed in public discourse. We speak of structural reforms across the board, but the grave issue of corruption is not viewed as a priority. While countries like New Zealand, Denmark, Finland, Norway, and Sweden rank high on the list of the most honest countries, Mexico finds itself plagued by corruption. Ethical nations, as

---

65 http://transparencia.org.es/wp-content/uploads/2016/01/comparacion_ipc-2007_a_2015.pdf

2015 CORRUPTION PERCEPTION INDEX

Bloc/Region	Mexico's position				Evaluated countries total			
	2012	2013	2014	2015	2012	2013	2014	2015
America	20	20	18	14	30	30	29	24
Latin America	11	11	10	10	20	20	20	20
Latin America and the Caribbean	19	20	17	12	28	28	27	22
G20	17	16	16	17	19	19	19	19
OECD	34	34	34	34	34	34	34	34
BRICS + Mexico	5	5	5	5	6	6	6	6
Global Ranking	106	106	103	95	176	177	175	168

Source: Corruption Perception Index 2015, Transparency International.

should be obvious, have a stronger middle class; they have largely eradicated poverty, instability, and violence.

When corruption is prevented, the state is able to promote development and meet its social responsibilities. Norway is the third largest exporter of petroleum in the world, and petroleum revenues are administered by the state for the benefit of the people. In states where democracy is robust, human rights are respected; universal access to the internet is guaranteed, and the welfare state alleviates inequality and aids social justice. In Denmark, for example, the population receives free comprehensive education, free medical care, old age pensions, rent assistance, six months' maternity leave, and free access to libraries and recreation centers. We, in Mexico, could accomplish the same if we root out corruption, and make the most of our wealth of natural resources and our hardworking people.

Honesty is not foreign to our people. It is central to Mexican society. Although things may seem thoroughly corrupted, the history of our people is built upon a bedrock of honesty. By nurturing our moral fiber, Mexico as a nation can harness our collective will for the benefit of all.

For this reason, our primary goal is to elevate honesty as a national virtue. Thankfully, the people of Mexico have a rich legacy in the Mesoamerican civilization, and we have a deep well of principles which can serve to revitalize our public life. We have communities where crops are stored openly in the fields, and where no one thinks to take what is not theirs. Until recently, many rural localities could not even conceive of theft. One anecdote comes to mind: recently, a young associate of MORENA[66] forgot his wallet aboard a flight and days later received a call from a migrant farmer from California to let him know that it had been found. The farmworker, hailing from Veracruz, mailed it to his home. My young associate asked the migrant, who barely spoke Spanish, why he did

---

66 The National Regeneration Movement, a left-oriented political party headed by AMLO.

it. The man replied that his parents had taught him to do good with no eye to whether there would be a reward.

Only when we return to our historic roots of honesty and fairness, and make them central tenets in our government, can we revitalize Mexico. When we are in power the perpetrators of systemic corruption will find no safe haven, nor will they benefit from unearned privileges. Such an ethical approach will allow us to redirect resources, today lost to corruption, toward the development of our nation and the well-being of our people.

Flying the flag of honesty will require the participation of public servants. Leading by example will be their most important role. Corruption is largely a top-down issue, and in combating it we, as leaders, must act transparently. A president committed to the fight against corruption will accomplish much more if the public servants around him or her share the same values.

We must have zero tolerance for those who believe they are above the law. Upon receiving the mandate of the people, I will reform the Constitution to ensure that everyone in power is held accountable, no matter his or her position. I will abolish the precept that the head of state is exempt from charges of corruption. This proposal stems from Article 103 of our 1857 Constitution: "Representatives of Congress, the Supreme Court and the Secretary General will be held accountable for any crimes, offenses, and omissions during their time in office. Governors of the States shall be equally accountable. The President, too, but during their term they may only be accused of treason, violation of the Constitution, attacks to electoral freedom, and other grave offenses."

As the Mexican Revolution raged, borne out of demands for justice and democracy, the Constituent Congress of 1917[67] enacted important social protections and strengthened our sovereignty. Unfortunately, they eliminated the 1857 precept that made the president of the Republic accountable for attacks on electoral freedom, and upheld the provision granting him immunity from prosecution for acts of corruption. As the end of President Manuel

---

67   Elected body convened to draft a new Mexican constitution.

González's term neared, Porfírio and his delegates accused him of corruption. Once González accepted Porfírio's re-election, these same representatives absolved him, with the ruling that as per Article 103 of the Constitution, the president can only be judged for treason, express violation of the Constitution, attacks on electoral liberties, and grave offenses. Today, just as in the past, this ruling stands, save for protections against voter suppression and violation of the Constitution; these provisions were recklessly eliminated in the Constitution of 1917.

As undemocratic reforms were implemented and widespread criminal impunity took hold, the corrupt presidentialist regime found its footing in post-revolution Mexico. Our tolerance for corruption is a grave embarrassment when one considers how other countries deal with it. Look at Guatemala: their ex-president was imprisoned for fraudulently appropriating 40 million pesos (US$2.1 million), while in Mexico, heads of state have stolen far more than that without any meaningful consequences. This former president of Guatemala is a mere pickpocket when compared to our own band of corrupt politicians. With this in mind, we will put forward a proposal to amend Article 108 of the Constitution in order to hold the head of state and other higher-ups accountable under the same laws that they profess to enforce.

*

The enormous task of transforming Mexico will only be addressed by men and women with moral and political authority. We need genuine public servants, guided by values higher than ambition, who are capable of understanding that power is only virtuous when it's wielded in the service of the people. Our selection of cabinet members will be based on this criteria, with no eye to political affiliation.

The government must lead by example if we are to combat corruption. Public servants must be steadfast in their honesty; no one who intends to fill private coffers with public funds will find a place in our administration. Participation in government must not be seen as an opportunity to do business and enrich oneself at the expense of the state. We must repair our poor public image. Once freed of corruption, the federal government will be able to command moral and political authority on the world stage.

In sum:

A) We will call upon the people to honor and respect honesty as a central virtue, since our vision and our values depend on the participation of the Mexican people.

B) We will facilitate public participation in every step of the fight against corruption.

C) We will create streamlined and effective mechanisms to allow citizens to denounce corruption.

D) We will demand—and enforce—universal transparency. We will establish a legal authority to publish the assets and financial interests of the bureaucratic hierarchy, from top to bottom. We must ensure that a prompt process of accountability is established, since transparency means nothing if we cannot act upon that knowledge. All government functionaries must disclose their financial interests, which are to be cross-referenced for accuracy and certified. Any anomalies will be investigated.

E) Such investigations will be conducted promptly, in contrast to current practice where complaints take years to be investigated.

F) Domestic and foreign firms wishing to bid on public works projects or contracts or to utilize our natural resources, and who have former government functionaries in upper management, must wait for a minimum of ten years after the departure or retirement of said government functionaries before bidding.

G) Public servants and companies involved in the creation of overpriced contracts for public works will be charged under the relevant laws.

H) Government officials and their families will be barred from associating with foreign or domestic firms for the purpose of conducting private deals at the expense of the state.

I) Nepotism will not be tolerated. Public servants, contractors, suppliers, and leaders who benefit at the treasury's expense will have no place in our government.

J) Corruption, money laundering, and conflicts of interest will be charged as serious offenses and be subject to harsh penalties.

K) The Constitution will be reformed to create a Federal Judicial Authority that is fully autonomous, with ample power to combat corruption.

The eradication of corruption depends fundamentally upon the moral authority of the state, and a leader with the political will to pursue such a task. If our public servants act with integrity, and nepotism is outlawed, an efficiently managed budget will benefit society as a whole. But if shady associations between politicians and private industry continue to be tolerated, corruption will continue to be the hallmark of Mexican society. In January of 2015, the *Diario Oficial* published the 2016 budget and two months later, the treasury secretary, without any justification, increased the budgets of eight projects whose contractors had ties to federal officials. These projects had originally been approved by Congress with a budget of 189.3 billion pesos (US$10.3 billion). This was then increased to 286.1 billion (US$15.6 billion), an increase of more than 50 percent. One standout example was the case of the new Mexico City airport, which had been approved at 104.3 billion pesos (US$5.6 billion), and then increased to 180.1 billion pesos (US$9.8 billion), a 72.5 percent increase.

Three months later, in June 2016, the treasury secretary made cuts to public spending of 31 billion pesos due to the severe financial turmoil caused by Brexit. These cuts did not touch the aforementioned projects. Instead, it was public welfare programs which paid the price. Public health insurance, support for indigenous communities, farmers, scholarships and public education, the Prospera anti-poverty initiative, science and technology funding, water treatment and small business grants—all were cut.

The same is true of the 2017 budget—social programs were again the first to suffer. This state of affairs cannot go on. Ridding ourselves of the scourge of corruption would save up to 10 percent of the national budget—some 500 billion pesos (US$27.2 billion).

¡Oye, Trump! Speech 8

The Silent Complicity of Peña Nieto's Administration

New York City and Washington, D.C., March 14 and 15, 2017

Following my meeting with migrants in New York, we had scheduled an interview with the United Nation's High Commissioner for Human Rights of the United Nations. The meeting was postponed due to a winter storm but we still managed to deliver a formal letter of complaint to his office condemning discrimination against the Mexican people and the orders issued by Donald Trump to begin construction of the border wall and widen persecution of migrants more generally.

This complaint should have been presented by the Mexican government the moment those arbitrary measures, which violate the Universal Declaration of Human Rights to which all nations, including the US, are signatories, were taken. However, Peña Nieto's regime, lacking political and moral authority, permitted this affront to our people to go unchallenged.

The letter reads as follows:

Mr. Andrew Gilmour,
Assistant Secretary-General for Human Rights and Head of the Office of the High Commissioner for Human Rights

Dear Sir,

As the whole world is aware, the people of Mexico face a grave economic crisis as well as instability and violence.

This has resulted from the imposition of the neoliberal model derived from the so-called "Washington Consensus." Since that time, a small group of Mexicans and foreigners have dedicated themselves to pillaging the resources of Mexico and depriving the vast majority of the Mexican people of what is rightfully theirs, and thereby denying them any meaningful future.

This greedy minority cares nothing for the development of our country. The government—which exists to serve to serve the people—has created widespread poverty. Government support for our rural areas ceased; jobs were no longer created, and our young people were neglected. They have been deprived of the right to education and work. This explains, in large part, the widespread resentment and violence that has plagued my country for many years.

Faced with this crisis, and lacking any other options, millions of Mexicans have undertaken an exhausting and painful journey through the desert to cross the border into the United States in the hopes of making an honest living there.

Millions of Mexicans have been driven from our country due to privatization and unemployment. They migrated to lessen their hunger and poverty, and now face a climate of hatred and discrimination disseminated during the campaign of president Donald Trump.

The plans to construct a border wall and persecute migrants in this country are in violation of the Universal Declaration of Human Rights; the International Covenant on Civil and Political Rights; and the International Covenant on Economic, Social and Cultural Rights—fundamental documents signed by members of the UN, including the United States of America.

Based on the above, and given Enrique Peña Nieto's failure to act in the face of these threats, we have come to present this complaint and ask you to condemn the United States and call upon them to cease violating human rights and practicing racial discrimination.

We must not forget that that titan of liberty, President Franklin Delano Roosevelt, a champion and co-creator of the UN, proclaimed the four fundamental principles that went on to be codified in the Universal Declaration of Human Rights: freedom of speech, freedom of religion, the right to life, and the right to safety.

It's pertinent to contrast these four principles with the massive reversals in human rights spawned by Trump's politics of hate and chauvinism.

All human beings must raise their voices and confront racism, segregation, authoritarianism, and its most sinister expression of our time, neo-fascism.

The Statue of Liberty must not be an empty symbol, nor must the UN be a mere bureaucratic apparatus in a beautiful glass building.

Andrés Manuel López Obrador
National President of MORENA

On March 15, 2017, we arrived in Washington to formalize the complaint before the Inter-American Commission on Human Rights. The complaint, drafted by lawyer Netzaí Sandoval Ballesteros, was signed by more than eleven million Mexican and American citizens from all walks of life, religions, and ideologies including Father Alejandro Solalinde, the Mexican activist Nestora Salgado, the author Elena Poniatowska, the philosopher Enrique Dussel, the attorneys Marco A. Palau and John Burroughs, and a wide range of prominent academics.

The complaint seeks to challenge two executive orders issued on January 25, 2017, by President Trump, one titled "Enhancing Public Safety in the Interior of the United States" and the other "Border Security and Immigration Enforcement Improvements." We believe that these orders violate the presumption of innocence, disregard the right to asylum, ignore due process, and omit protections relevant to child migrants. They are discriminatory, equating grave crimes with minor offenses; they uphold the collective expulsion of foreigners without examining the specific circumstances in each case; and they trample over the concept of *jus cogens* (a principle of international law that is so fundamental that it binds all states and does not allow any for exceptions).

Additionally, these orders open the door to all foreigners being viewed as potentially deportable, whether or not they have been accused of a crime. Mere suspicion of any wrongdoing is now sufficient for immigration officers to take action.

The authority to which we are appealing has had jurisdiction over such matters since 1959 and can take decisive action if it chooses to. The United States of America is subject to its obligations under the American Declaration on the Rights and Duties of Man according to the Statute of the Inter-American Commission on Human Rights as set out in Articles 20 and 51.

In the past, the Mexican State has been proactive in securing the protection of its people, for example, by asserting their right to consular assistance. For this reason, we have initiated lawsuits before the International Court of Justice and sought advisory opinions from the Inter-American Court of Human Rights. Faced with the passive and ineffective response of the Mexican government, we, independent citizens of both Mexico and the United States, have made the decision to defend the rights of migrants from Mexico and all over the world.

CHAPTER 8

REPUBLICAN AUSTERITY

The idea that Mexico cannot invest in development for lack of funding has been widely disseminated. This is untrue. Mexico's public wealth, despite its steady decline throughout the neoliberal period, remains significant. State intervention should not hinder civil society, nor prevent cooperation between the public and private sectors. But it's another thing altogether to claim that the state cannot meet its responsibility to promote development.

The problem is corruption, not a lack of funds. In 2017, the budget authorized by the Chamber of Deputies was 4.9 billion pesos (US$267.2 million); that is to say, on average 13,000 pesos per month for each family (US$709). However, the vast majority of this budget is not invested in development or public welfare initiatives; rather, it facilitates the transfer of public goods to private hands. The budget is used to maintain an onerous bureaucratic structure that serves the political *mafiosi*.

A judicious budget is not merely a prudent administrative decision, but a moral imperative. Those in office, as President Juárez said, "must not use funds irresponsibly; they must not govern impulsively, but through measured application of the law; they must not make fortunes nor surrender to idleness and gratification, but dedicate themselves diligently to work, resigned to live honorably off the remuneration provided under the law." Let me

REALLOCATION OF RESOURCES

Millions of Pesos (Billions of US Dollars).

Allocation	Approved 2016	Adjusted 2016	Approved 2017	Proposed 2017
Net public sector expenditures	4,763,874 (261)	4,602,296(255)	4,888,893 (268)	4,888,893 (268)
Non-programmable costs	1,157,168 (64)	1,157,168 (64)	1,338,505 (73)	1,333,505 (73)
Interest payments [1]	462,372 (25)	462,372 (25)	572,563 (31)	567,563 (31)
Federal funds to the states	678,747 (37)	678,747 (37)	742,566 (41)	742,566 (41)
ADEFAS (Debts from the previous tax year)	16,049 (1)	16,049 (1)	23,376 (1)	23,376 (1)
Programmable costs	3,606,706 (198)	3,445,128 (189)	3,550,388 (195)	3,555,388 (195)
Recurrent expenditures	2,867,837 (157)	2,816,261 (155)	2,964,989 (163)	2,608,323 (143)
Investment	738,869 (41)	628,867 (35)	585,399 (32)	947,064 (52)

1   Includes expenditures by the Secretary of Finance and Public Credit towards Branch 34, Expenditures to Support Savings and Debt Relief of 20.5 billion pesos approved and adjusted in 2016, and approved for 35.8 billion pesos in 2017.
Source: Federal Budget for the Fiscal Years of 2016 and 2017; for the adjusted 2016 budget we called upon two cuts announced by the state. The budget excludes subsidies and transfers from the Federal Government to entities under direct control and state owned entities, as well as contributions to ISSSTE (Institute for Social Security and Services).

add that there must be no rich public servants so long as the people are poor.

A politics of austerity would allow us—once corruption has been addressed—to invest in the development and the well-being of our people. With this strategy, there will be no need to raise taxes in real terms or to create new taxes; neither would we have to bankroll the state through financing and debt.

How do we do it?

To free up and reassign funds, we would implement the following measures:

We would save 5 billion pesos (US$272.7 million) in interest payments through the following:

A) The government will commit to strengthening our fiscal position by pledging to live within our means by creating balanced budgets.

B) Fostering trust in the safety of investments; their profits will create a climate more conducive to lowering interest rates and securing more attractive refinancing terms.

C) The reduction we propose is very conservative. Consider this: in September 2016, the net public debt of the Public Sector Budget was 9.2 trillion pesos (US$501.8 billion), and nearly 480 billion pesos (US$26.1 billion) would go toward interest, commissions, and debt spending by the year's close. The official 2017 budget allocates 568 billion pesos (US$30.9 billion) toward these expenses.

D) Throughout the negotiations to restructure the federal debt, the Bank of Mexico will take an active role as the financial agent and advisor to the federal government.

E) This institution will be asked to weigh in on public spending, with an eye toward protecting our economy from inflation.

To reduce running expenditures, we propose cuts from Chapter 1000 of the budget, dubbed "Personal Services," which amounts to 1.1 trillion pesos (US$60 billion). We would cut this sum by 11 percent, or 132 billion pesos (US$7.2 billion). Most of this sum currently goes toward salaries and discretionary payments. At present, there is no transparency regarding the true income of public officials; the real figures are hidden behind bonuses. In 2017, there are 1,766,191 public servants employed, earning a combined 740 billion pesos (US$40.3 billion), 64 percent of the total cost of "Personal Services." We shall implement full economic transparency in each branch of the federal government, in keeping with Article 127 of the Constitution.

Millions of Pesos (Billions of US Dollars)

Field	Description	Position	Annual cost of salaries analyzed by position	Annual cost of itemized budget	Variation
	Total	1,766,191 (97)	740,043 (41)	825,660 (45)	85,617 (5)
1	Legislative Branch	6,913 (0.4)	4,609 (0.3)	8,898 (0.5)	4,289 (0.2)
2	Office of the President of the Republic	1,307 (0.1)	705 (0.04)	1,044 (0.1)	339 (0.02)
3	Judicial Branch	46,869 (3)	50,266 (3)	54,775 (3)	4,509 (0.2)
4	Secretariat of the Interior	79,867 (4)	32,352 (2)	32,252 (2)	-100 (-0.01)
5	Secretariat of Foreign Affairs	3,703 (0.2)	1,818 (0.1)	4,848 (0.3)	3,030 (0.2)
6	Secretariat of Finance and Public Credit	43,009 (2)	17,131 (1)	17,011(1)	-120 (-0.01)
7	Secretariat of National Defense	214,325 (12)	62,230 (3)	51,145 (3)	-11,085 (-1)
8	Secretariat of Agriculture, Livestock, Rural Development, Fishing, and Food	22,453 (1)	7,509 (0.4)	7,535 (0.4)	25 (0.001)
9	Secretariat of Communications and Transportation	19,553 (1)	6,826 (0.4)	7,286(0.4)	459 (0.03)
10	Secretariat of Economy	6,738 (0.4)	2,685 (0.1)	3,098 (0.2)	413 (0.02)

11	Secretariat of Public Education	199,800 (11)	72,441 (4)	101,519 (6)	29,078 (2)
12	Secretariat of Health	67,813 (4)	24,615 (1)	25,666 (1)	1,015 (0.1)
13	Secretariat of the Navy	65,605 (4)	22,191 (1)	19,516 (1)	-2,675 (-0.1)
14	Secretariat of Labor and Social Welfare	5,811 (0.3)	1,981 (0.1)	2,054 (0.1)	74 (0.004)
15	Secretariat of Agrarian, Land, and Urban Development	6,133 (0.3)	1,992 (0.1)	1,863 (0.1)	-129 (-0.01)
16	Secretariat of Environment and Natural Resources	23,206 (1)	7,428 (0.4)	7,888 (0.4)	461 (0.03)
17	Office of the Attorney General	25,918 (1)	12,392 (1)	11,618 (1)	-774 (-0.04)
18	Secretariat of Energy	3,032 (0.2)	1,842 (0.1)	1,519 (0.1)	-324 (-0.02)
20	Secretariat of Social Development	10,917 (1)	3,646 (0.2)	2,914 (0.2)	-733 (-0.04)
21	Secretariat of Tourism	2,185 (0.1)	965 (0.1)	984 (0.1)	19 (0.001)
22	National Electoral Institute	10,538 (1)	4,864 (0.3)	7,373 (0.4)	2,509 (0.1)
23	Economic and Salary Provisions	2,705 (0.1)	657 (0.04)	19,336 (1)	18,679 (1)
25	Federal Administration for Educational Services	98,646 (5)	22,731 (1)	49,986 (3)	27,255 (1)
27	Secretariat of the Civil Service	1,734 (0.1)	1,100 (0.1)	869 (0.05)	-231 (-0.01)
31	Agrarian Courts	1,611 (0.1)	671 (0.04)	614 (0.03)	-57 (-0.003)
32	Federal Court of Fiscal and Administrative Justice	3,253 (0.2)	1,904 (0.1)	1,976 (0.1)	72 (0.004)
35	National Commission Of Human Rights	1,689 (0.1)	1,149 (0.1)	1,263 (0.1)	113 (0.01)
37	Judicial Council of the Executive Branch	159 (0.01)	126 (0.01)	107 (0.01)	-19 (-0.001)

38	National Council for Science and Technology	8,216 (0.5)	5,065 (0.3)	5,529 (0.3)	464 (0.03)
40	National Institute of Statistics and Geography	13,629 (1)	4,571 (0.3)	5,455 (0.3)	884 (0.05)
41	Federal Economic Competition Commission	448 (0.02)	398 (0.02)	419 (0.02)	21 (0.001)
42	National Institute for Educational Assessment	778 (0.04)	531 (0.03)	530 (0.03)	-2 (-0.0001)
43	Federal Telecommunications Institute	1,263 (0.1)	932 (0.1)	935 (0.1)	3 (0.0002)
44	Federal Institute for Access to Public Information	709 (0.04)	641 (0.04)	670 (0.04)	29 (0.002)
45	Energy Regulatory Commission	235 (0.01)	235 (0.01)	238 (0.01)	3 (0.0002)
46	National Hydrocarbons Commission	214 (0.01)	233 (0.01)	219 (0.01)	-14 (-0.001)
47	Non-compartmentalized entities	3,738 (0.2)	1,460 (0.1)	1,630 (0.1)	169 (0.01)
48	Secretariat of Culture	13,792 (1)	4,610 (0.3)	5,532 (0.3)	922 (0.1)
50	Mexican Social Security Institute	430,258 (24)	183,882 (10)	176,493 (10)	-7,389 (-0.4)
51	Institute for Social Security and Services for State Workers	106,426 (6)	35,361 (2)	38,286 (2)	2,925 (0.2)
52	Pemex	116,601 (6)	77,125 (4)	89,813 (5)	12,688 (1)
53	Federal Electricity Commission	94,392 (5)	56,170 (3)	54,953 (3)	-1,217 (-0.1)

Note: excluding 64,574 job slots from the Direct Control Entities which do not form part of the Personnel Services Chapter, and the Index of Codes; item number 33 is excluded in order to ensure a fair comparison. In the case of Medical Doctors (other than Family Doctors)**** of the IMSS, the ordinary numbers count from 2016 are used, given that 2017 numbers are inexplicably lower by 56%.

Source: Federal Expense Budget for Fiscal 2017, Volume IX Job Slots and Pay Listing: Budget Transparency, Open Data, Index of Job Codes.

We will seek an incremental and proportional reduction in the salaries of department heads and higher ranking officials. The cuts will be smaller for middle-ranking officials, and will increase for those on higher salaries. For example, the president, secretaries, representatives, senators, magistrates, and judges, who earn over 220,000 pesos per month (US$12,000), will earn a maximum net salary of 110,000 pesos (US$6,000). High-ranking functionaries are dramatically overpaid. Our country's bureaucrats have gained notoriety worldwide for inflated salaries that take up a huge proportion of our budget and are often greater than those in the private sector.

In 2016, the only member of the US government to earn more than Mexico's high-ranking officials was President Barack Obama. All of our Supreme Court judges, judiciary council members, and the president of the Federal Electoral Tribunal commanded larger salaries than the presidents and prime ministers of Canada, Germany, Sweden, the UK, Japan, South Africa, Chile, Brazil, and Italy.

According to official data, the salaries of high-ranking officials in 2017 are listed on page 115.

Alongside stratospheric wages, our bureaucratic elites enjoy lavish private medical care, with some functionaries treating themselves to plastic surgery on the treasury's dime. They have retirement funds and access to cheap credit for auto and home purchases. Paradoxically, they have attempted to justify their inflated salaries by claiming that generous pay makes them more efficient and incorruptible, when in practice the opposite is true. In a country where the vast majority lives in poverty, anyone who would accept those sums of money and privileges for public service is fundamentally dishonest.

The myth that private sector leaders earn more than public officials is wholly unsubstantiated. The directors of Sanborns, Coca-Cola, Bimbo, banks, and real estate developers earn less than half of what cabinet secretaries make and less than a third of what Supreme Court justices take home. In 2010, the average monthly public sector wage was 23,456 pesos (US$1,279); however, this

SALARIES OF HIGH RANKING OFFICIALS IN OTHER COUNTRIES
Pesos (Thousands of US Dollars)

Country	President	Minister of Justice		Secretary of State	Congressman	Senator
US	7,224,000 (396)	4,708,242 (258)		4,292,862 (236)	3,142,440 (172)	3,492,804 (192)
Canada	6,287,280 (345)	2,433,356.60 (134)		857,050 (47)	2,394,120 (131)	2,042,870 (112)
Germany	4,358,840 (239)	3,669,033.60 (201)		3,731,495 (205)	2,420,681 (133)	1,107,031 (61)
Mexico	4,300,854 (236)	6,766,428 (371)	1	3,672,546 (202)	1,916,121 (105)	2,732,992 (150)
South Africa	4,157,100 (228)	3,688,756.20 (202)		3,148,920.90 (173)	2,460,511.68 (135)	3,148,920.90 (173)
Sweden	4,126,670 (226)	-		4,153,040.40 (228)	1,620,120 (89)	2,538,108 (139)
UK	3,975,750 (218)	6,072,780 (333)		2,754,846 (151)	2,091,440 (115)	2,549,112.19 (140)
Chile	3,637,155 (200)	1,715,024.79 (94)		3,235,692 (178)	2,334,061 (128)	3,235,692 (178)
Brazil	3,625,724 (199)	2,390,600.33 (131)		1,431,360 (79)	3,241,800 (178)	1,515,254.16 (83)
Italy	2,079,963 (114)	1,120,977.97 (62)		-	2,867,332 (157)	2,426,129.66 (133)

1 In 2016, the President of the Supreme Court of Justice, judiciary council members, and the president of the Supreme Electoral Tribunal had the same salary.
http://usgovinfo.about.com/od/governmentjobs/a/Annual-Salaries-Of-Top-Us-Government-Officials.htm
http://www.lop.parl.gc.ca/ParlInfo/Lists/Salaries.aspx?Menu=HOC-Politic&Section=b571082f-7b2d-4d6a-b30a-b6025a9cbb98&Year=2016
http://www.abc.es/20120603/internacional/abci-sueldos-presidentes-ministros-europa-201205292201.html
http://www.eleconomista.es/economia/noticias/1252253/05/09/Cuanto-gana-un-diputado-en-los-paiseseuropeos.html
http://www.theclinic.cl/2015/03/11/el-sueldo-de-bachelet-en-comparacion-con-los-presidentes-de-las-potencias-mundiales/
http://spanish.peopledaily.com.cn/31614/7890757.html
http://www.riksdagen.se/en/how-the-riksdag-works/the-work-of-the-riksdag/the-members/
http://www.parliament.uk/documents/lords-finance-office/2014-15/Financial-support-for-Members-briefingnote-2014-15.pdf
http://www.abc.es/20120603/internacional/abci-sueldos-presidentes-ministros-europa-201205292201.html
http://www.theclinic.cl/2015/03/11/el-sueldo-de-bachelet-en-comparacion-con-los-presidentes-de-las-potencias-mundiales/
http://www.lasegunda.com/Noticias/Nacional/2014/04/927550/sueldos-de-diputados-chilenos-entre-los-mas-altos-del-continente-polemica-por-proyecto-para-rebajarlos
http://www6g.senado.leg.br/transparencia/sen/4981/?ano=2016
http://cnnespanol.cnn.com/2016/11/01/venezuela-el-pais-donde-los-congresistas-tienen-el-salario-mas-bajo/
http://www.theclinic.cl/2015/03/11/el-sueldo-de-bachelet-en-comparacion-con-los-presidentes-de-las-potencias-mundiales/
http://www.eleconomista.es/economia/noticias/1252253/05/09/Cuanto-gana-un-diputado-en-los-paiseseuropeos.html
NOTE: We used the following exchange rate: Pesos/EUR 20.21; Pesos/Dollar 18.06; Pesos/Swedish krona 2.13; Pesos/South African Rand 1.35; Peso/Brazilian Real 5.68; Peso/Canadian Dollar 13.98; Peso/Chilean Peso 0.27

SALARIES OF HIGH RANKING OFFICIALS IN MEXICO
Pesos (Thousands of US Dollars)

Remuneration	President of the Republic	Senator	Congressman	Federal Superior Auditor	President of the Supreme Court	Judiciary Council	President of the Supreme Electoral Tribunal	Magistrate of the Electoral Tribunal	President of the Federal Electoral Institute	President of the National Commission Of Human Rights
Annual Net Compensation	3,002,972 (165)	1,884,312 (103)	1,460,550 (80)	2,957,059 (162)	4,658,775 (256)	4,714,413 (259)	4,564,875 (251)	2,961,450 (163)	2,994,563 (164)	2,905,378 (159)
Income tax (35%)*	1,311,726 (72)	850,783 (47)	482,361 (26)	1,307,710 (72)	2,279,459 (125)	2,223,821 (122)	2,201,553 (121)	1,342,447 (74)	1,298,266 (71)	1,320,054 (72)
Annual Gross Compensation	4,314,698 (237)	2,735,095 (150)	1,942,911 (107)	4,264,769 (234)	6,938,234 (381)	6,938,234 (381)	6,766,428 (371)	4,303,897 (236)	4,292,829 (236)	4,225,432 (232)
I. Ordinary Compensations:	3,460,475 (190)	2,735,095 (150)	1,942,911 (107)	3,438,058 (189)	6,085,011 (334)	6,085,011 (334)	5,955,833 (327)	3,615,142 (198)	4,292,929 (236)	3,459,626 (190)
a) Salary and wages:	2,502,851 (137)	2,057,328 (113)	1,264,536 (69)	2,371,930 (130)	4,745,537 (260)	4,700,524 (258)	4,594,460 (252)	2,646.420 (145)	3,152,808 (173)	2,383,700 (131)
b) Benefits:	957,624 (53)	677,767 (37)	678,375 (37)	1,066,128 (59)	1,341,474 (74)	1,384,487 (76)	1,361,373 (75)	968,722 (53)	1,140,021 (63)	1,075,926 (59)
II. Special Compensations:	854,223 (47)	-	-	826,711 (45)	853,223 (47)	853,223 (47)	810,595 (44)	688,755 (38)	-	765,806 (42)
a) Life insurance and hazard pay 1	854,223 (47)	-	-	826,711 (45)	853,223 (47)	853,223 (47)	810,595 (44)	688,755 (38)	-	765,806 (42)

Source: Budget for the 2017 Fiscal Year.
* Calculated according to income tax law.
1 Corresponds to contributions towards life insurance and hazard pay, which makes up 30% of ordinary monthly remuneration, through wages and salaries, in terms of Article 19, Section II, subparagraph b) of this decree.

figure is misleadingly inflated: the average salary of Social Security recipients was a mere 6,888 pesos per month (US$375). That same year, the American Chamber of Commerce surveyed private industry in Mexico and discovered that the average monthly income of a general manager was 89,808 pesos ($4,899 US$), while a mid-career government functionary received 143,297 pesos per month (US$7,816). Just by adjusting the inflated salaries of public servants, we would save 70 billion pesos (US$3.8 billion).

From Chapter 1000 of the budget, we propose the elimination of entry 14404, titled "Individualized Separation Insurance." It consists of a savings account wherein the functionary deposits a certain amount each month, and the government matches the amount. Thus, when the functionary retires or changes careers, he or she takes those savings.

In 2017 this program cost the treasury an exorbitant 8.9 billion pesos (US$485 million). We also propose to eliminate medical expense insurance that is granted to high-ranking functionaries (entry 14403), which in 2017 cost our country 4.3 billion pesos (US$234 million).

Our proposal includes a new framework for governance that is centered on strategic development projects. We will put an end to costly and inefficient duplication of efforts across government agencies and focus on programs with a demonstrable impact on the economy and on the well-being of our people. We will get rid of needless bureaucracy. To begin with, we will request that the nineteen secretaries of state keep on only 30 percent of their senior staff. The 2017 payroll currently includes sub-secretaries, officials, mayors, general coordinators, delegates, general directors, directors, and advisors, amounting to a total of 6,244 people. Under my plan, this would be reduced to 1,827 people. It's important to note that between 2012 and 2017 there was an increase of 27,885 executive positions in the public sector, each earning over 1 million pesos per year (US$54,550). Our austerity plan would eliminate superfluous positions, allowing us to save 13.8 billion pesos (US$753 million).

Another avenue for freeing up funds for development is changing government procurement procedures in order to save on goods and services. In February 2012, the Organisation for Economic Co-operation and Development (OECD) noted that if Mexico were to revisit its purchasing procedures, it could save 120 billion pesos (US$6.5 billion). Around the same time, at its Global Forum on Competition, which took place in March 2012, the OECD estimated that corruption and bribery cost nearly 100 billion pesos (US$5.4 billion), between 7 and 10 percent of the state's total purchases.

Government officials are getting unconscionably rich at the expense of the state. In Mexico, we hear of *mordidas*[68] given to transit officers; police collusion with violent gangs; and other cases that negatively affect our citizens' quality of life. But the most severe corruption happens in the halls of political and economic power. Beyond the plundering of our treasury, the neoliberal model provides cover for a whole host of corrupt practices that take a cumulative toll on our economy. We see it in the acquisition of goods, leases, and services, the management of public works, in public-private partnerships, financing schemes, in the handover of grants and subsidies to private firms, in shady trusts . . . the list goes on.

In acquisitions, leases, and public works, we see illegal commissions for high-ranking officials who manage the bidding processes and assign contracts. These bribes are often 10 percent to 20 percent of the overall cost.

In addition to these clandestine payments, companies often must offer "other support," which adds up to another 5 percent of contracted imports: payments to officials who manage appraisals, to those who authorize the weight of shipments, and to those who receive the goods and make the payments. In short, resources are depleted through these corrupt practices, making up to 25 percent of contractor costs. This, needless to say, affects the quality of their output and the general competitiveness of our economy.

68   Bribes.

117

Often, government functionaries tasked with receiving ship-ments allow suppliers to deliver less than was promised in exchange for a bribe. This is all too common in the acquisition of medical sup-plies. In the absence of strict inventory control practices, receivers often skim off the top, selling these products on the black market at the expense of poor communities with limited access to medicine. Another common scam is to request maintenance on equipment that does not require it. A contractor is assigned, who "repairs" it and then returns it to the institution, charging for a service that was not needed in the first place. Collusion between government officials and contractors has become dangerously entrenched.

Illicit kickbacks are pervasive in the world of government purchasing and contracting. These are fairly common scams, but they're not inherently difficult to address. Corruption of this nature can be eliminated with relative ease the moment a president refuses to sanction it. A head of state willing to stand up in defense of the treasury would lay the foundations for a culture of honesty across government and society.

Through the suppression of theft, bribery, price gouging, inefficiency, and poor quality provision of public works, goods, and services, we could eliminate an estimated 120 billion pesos (US$6.5 billion) in waste. We certainly have the requisite experience to govern openly and honestly. For instance, in 2002, the Mexico City government invested 7.5 billion pesos (US$409 million) in the city's rail system. Expanding capacity was an urgent necessity, as no new trains had been purchased in a decade. A system trans-porting 4,500,000 people per day had only 300 trains. We decided to increase capacity by 17 percent, adding an additional 45 trains and 405 subway cars. To avoid the embarrassing debacles of the past, this sizeable acquisition was made with utmost transpar-ency. A number of prominent public figures were invited to over-see the process: Froylán López Narváez,[69] Elena Gallegos,[70] Katia

---

69 Journalist at *Milenio*, one of the leading papers.

70 Journalist at *El Universal,* winner of the 1998 National Journalism Award.

D'Artigues,[71] Rogelio Ramírez de la O,[72] Horacio Labastida,[73] Luis Alejandro Ferrer Argote,[74] Juan Manuel Arriaga,[75] and Baltasar Mena Iniesta.[76] The contract was assigned to Bombardier, which committed to build the trains at its plant in Ciudad Sahagún, Hidalgo, thereby creating jobs in Mexico. The savings, compared to previous acquisitions, were over 50 percent.

Public participation and citizen oversight is crucial in the assignment of contracts and acquisitions. In addition, we propose streamlining the procedures for government acquisition of goods and services. Much of this purchasing currently goes through subcontractors. With centralized purchasing in bulk, we estimate that at least 20 percent of federal agency purchases, including medical supplies, fuel, and office supplies could be made much more cheaply.

We will also save by cutting back on purchases of ships, planes, and helicopters. We'll sell the flotilla of planes and helicopters currently reserved for high-ranking officials, including those for use by the president; we will keep only those used for medical emergencies, security, and public safety. The president will travel by land and by commercial airlines.

During Calderón's term, and so far throughout Peña Nieto's, planes, helicopters, and ships have been acquired for the army, the marines, and the Attorney General's Office at a cost of around 85 billion pesos (US$4.6 billion). These purchases have been so high profile that the French government invited Peña Nieto and his defense secretary to a military parade in hopes of selling them a new fleet of helicopters. Besides a presidential plane costing 7.5 billion pesos (US$409 million), this administration bought luxury aircraft

71 Journalist at *El Universal*.

72 Mexican economist.

73 Author and historian.

74 Mechanical engineer.

75 Chairman of the National Chamber of Commerce of Mexico City.

76 Mechanical engineer; winner of the National Prize for Arts and Sciences (1997) and the UNESCO Science Prize (2001).

AIR FLOTILLA ACQUIRED BY PEÑA AND CALDERÓN
Millions of Pesos (Millions of US dollars)

Branch	Key figures portfolio	Project	Total Cost	Payment in previous years	Approved 2016	Modified September 2016	Approved 2017
		Total	84,926 (4661)	29,656 (1,627)	6,269 (344)	6,662 (366)	4,231 (232)
National Defense		Acquisition of planes for tactical operations	9,453 (519)	9,225 (506)	2,203 (121)	2,581 (142)	6 (0.3)
National Defense		Acquisition of 6 ec-725 helicopters for high impact operations, through lease	8,704 (478)	2,444 (134)	360 (20)	362 (20)	360 (20)
National Defense		Acquisition of strategic transport aircraft for Presidential use	7,215(391)	1,357 (74)	451 (25)	456 (25)	451 (25)
National Defense		Acquisition of c-295 planes configured for military transport	7,157 (393)	2,540 (139)	300 (16)	301 (17)	300 (16)
National Defense		Acquisition of 3 planes for aerial operations of aerial squadrons 201, 203, 204	6,935 (381)	983 (54)	427 (23)	436 (24)	427 (23)
Marines		Acquisition of aircraft for substantive operations	5,824 (320)	205 (11)	120 (7)	120 (7)	285 (16)
National Defense		Acquisition of airplanes to strengthen aerial transport capacity in aerial squadron 502	4,465 (245)	294 (16)	263 (14)	240 (13)	282 (15)

Marines	Acquisition of search and rescue aircraft	3,233 (177)	2,470 (136)	591 (32)	625 (34)	495 (27)
National Defense	Aquisition of fixed-wing aircraft to replace those older than 30 years	3,152 (173)	457 (25)	191 (10)	194 (11)	191 (10)
Marines	Acquisition of personal and cargo transport helicopters	3,131 (172)	1,167 (64)	174 (10)	174 (10)	174 (10)
National Defense	Aquisition of training aircraft for the military school of aviation	2,815 (154)	411 (23)	173 (9)	174 (10)	173 (9)
Marines	Acquisition of assets for surveillance operations	2,377 (130)	231 (13)	149 (8)	149 (8)	149 (8)
Marines	Acquisition of military transport and cargo aircraft	2,244 (123)	943 (52)	120 (7)	120 (7)	120 (7)
National Defense	Acquisition of 10 training aircrafts for military education	2,270 (125)	877 (48)	-	-	-
National Defense	Acquisition of planes for aerial operations for Aerial Squadron 402 of the Mexican Air Force	2,099 (115)	1,755 (96)	-	-	-
Marines	Acquisition of assets for substantive operations	2,013 (110)	100 (5)	65 (4)	65 (4)	134 (7)
Marines	Acquisition of personal and cargo transport airplanes	1,926 (106)	190 (10)	122 (7)	122 (7)	122 (7)

National Defense	Acquisition of plane for transport activities for E.A. 301	1,814 (100)	194 (11)	116 (6)	112 (6)	116 (6)
National Defense	Acquisition of 14 helicopters to modernize and reinforce the ESCA 111 fleet	1,799 (99)	265 (15)	109 (6)	111 (6)	109 (6)
National Defense	Acquisition of plane to reinforce capacity for transporting personnel	1,361 (75)	1,265 (69)	-	0	-
Marines	Acquisition of personal and cargo transport helicopters	1,088 (60)	874 (48)	178 (10)	178 (10)	181 (10)
Marines	Acquisition of training aircraft	915 (50)	296 (16)	-	-	-
Marines	Acquisition of aircraft for maritime surveillance	1,062 (58)	661 (36)	-	-	-
Marines	Acquisition of assets for logistical support	807 (44)	113 (6)	49 (3)	49 (3)	49 (3)
Marines	Acquisition of an aircraft for transport operations	682 (37)	95 (5)	41 (2)	41 (2)	41 (2)
Attorney General's Office	Acquisition of assets for substantive operations	386 (21)	244 (13)	67 (4)	53 (3)	67 (4)

Source: Budget for the 2016-2017 Fiscal Year, Volume VIII "Investment Programs and Projects" and quarterly reports on economic status, finances, and the public debt, "Physical and Financial Progress on Investment Programs and Projects."

LINE ITEM 33701 "PUBLIC SAFETY AND NATIONAL DEFENSE EXPENDITURES 2014-2017"
Millions of pesos (Millions of US dollars)

Branch	Description of Branch	Approved 2014	Fiscal Year 2014	Approved 2015	Fiscal Year 2015	Approved 2016	Modified June 2016	Approved 2017
		(1)	(2)	(3)	(4)	(5)	(6)	(7)
	Total	723 (40)	9,534 (523)	561 (31)	8,546 (469)	407 (22)	6,196 (340)	389 (21)
4	Governance	172 (9)	7,471 (410)	185 (10)	7,185 (394)	4 (0.2)	5,399 (296)	4 (0.2)
13	Marines	37 (2)	414 (23)	37 (2)	727 (40)	42 (2)	363 (20)	42 (2)
17	Attorney General	486 (27)	1,616 (89)	311 (17)	572 (31)	333 (18)	390 (21)	318 (17)
7	National Defense	22(1)	22 (1)	22 (1)	23 (1)	23 (1)	23 (1)	23 (1)
2	Office of the President	-	11 (1)	-	20 (1)	-	6 (0.3)	-
6	Secretariat of Finance	5 (0.3)	0	5 (0.3)	19 (1)	4 (0.2)	14 (1)	1 (0.1)
27	Secretariat of the Civil Service	1 (0.05)	0	1 (0.1)	1 (0.1)	1 (0.1)	1 (0.1)	1 (0.1)

Source: 2014-2015 Public Finance Accounts and Budget for the 2016-2017 Fiscal Year. Modifications to June 2017 refer to analytics provided by the Secretariat of Finance to the Chamber of Deputies

LINE ITEM 33104 "CONSULTS FOR PROGRAM OPERATIONS" 2014-2017
Millions of pesos (Millions of US dollars)

Branch	Description of Branch	Approved 2014 (1)	Fiscal Year 2014 (2)	Approved 2015 (3)	Fiscal Year 2015 (4)	Approved 2016 (5)	Modified June 2016 (6)	Approved 2017 (7)
	Total	4,735.1 (260)	6,236.1 (342)	5,882.3 (323)	8,375.4 (460)	5,729.0 (314)	6,666.8 (366)	4,205.9 (231)
52	Pemex	1,407.3 (77)	2,437.1 (134)	2,579.4 (142)	3,435.5 (189)	2,533.6 (139)	1,771 (97)	1,387.7 (76)
53	Federal Electricity Commission	640.5 (35)	840 (46)	869 (48)	1,085.1 (60)	1,347.3 (74)	1,271.8 (70)	1,347.3 (74)
15	Secretariat of Agrarian, Land, and Urban Development	25 (1)	328.7 (18)	47 (3)	392.4 (22)	30.5 (2)	121.6 (7)	21 (1)
16	Secretariat of Environment and Natural Resources	371.3 (20)	346.1 (19)	315.5 (17)	366.5 (20)	108.4 (6)	362.1 (20)	98.2 (5)
8	Secretariat of Agriculture, Livestock, Rural Development, Fisheries and Food	43.5 (2)	301.4 (17)	31.8 (2)	363.5 (20)	23.2 (1)	147.5 (8)	22.9 (1)
9	Secretariat of Communications and Transportation	236.8 (13)	222.9 (12)	245.9 (13)	328.4 (18)	195.7 (11)	429.9 (24)	135 (7)

Source: 2014-2015 Public Finance Accounts and Budget for the 2016-2017 Fiscal Year. Modifications to June 2017 refer to analytics provided by the Secretariat of Finance to the Chamber of Deputies.

51	Institute for Social Security and Services for State Workers	149.3 (8)	79.8 (4)	159 (9)	279.3 (15)	85.9 (5)	324.2 (18)	57.8 (3)
11	Secretariat of Public Education	683.7 (38)	342.7 (19)	313.4 (17)	239.9 (13)	213.5 (12)	314.7 (17)	84.9 (5)
27	Secretariat of the Civil Service	7.7 (0.4)	160.2 (9)	4.3 (0.2)	329.3 (18)	0.7 (0.04)	147 (8)	0.5 (0.03)
6	Secretariat of Finance	157.8 (9)	144.5 (8)	131.5 (7)	215.6 (12)	27.3 (1)	141.1 (8)	71.1 (4)
50	Mexican Social Security Institute	111.6 (6)	114.1 (6)	252.1 (14)	192.3 (11)	296.9 (16)	329.3 (18)	306.8 (17)
5	Secretariat of Foreign Affairs	54.5 (3)	76 (4)	58.5 (3)	171.6 (9)	38.1 (2)	246.4 (14)	18 (1)
20	Secretariat of Social Development	39.7 (2)	53.5 (3)	38.4 (2)	127.6 (7)	27.2 (1)	85.4 (5)	15.4 (1)
	Other	806.5 (44)	788.9 (43)	839.7 (46)	945.7 (52)	800.8 (44)	974.7 (53)	639.1 (35)

Source: 2014–2015 Public Finance Accounts and Budget for the 2016–2017 Fiscal Year. Modifications to June 2017 refer to analytics provided by the Secretariat of Finance to the Chamber of Deputies.

for the exclusive use of the defense secretary and former attorney general, Murillo Karam. These aircraft were valued at 1.5 billion pesos (US$81.8 million) each.

We will further eliminate needless spending by reducing operating costs (rent, office space, remodeling, broadcasts, trips, communications systems, and computation). We will limit official trips abroad, and restrict travel expenditures. We will save on the line items "Public and National Security Spending" (33104) and "Other Consultation for Program Operations" (33104). These appropriations are currently shrouded in secrecy. However, we've seen that in 2015 a budget of 185 million pesos (US$10 million) was authorized for them, yet actual spending was 7.1 billion pesos (US$387 million). Examples abound of irregularities of this sort under the Peña Nieto administration.

As for line item "Other Consultation for Program Operation," over half of this budget went directly to Pemex and the Federal Electricity Committee.

Needless to say, neoliberal technocracy has led to partiality with respect to hiring, and always at the expense of unions. There have been massive waves of firings and the implementation of so-called "voluntary retirement" programs. Nepotistic hiring has increased like never before, with well-connected staff receiving consistently higher salaries than union employees. In 2016, Pemex's payroll was 71.4 billion pesos (US$3.8 billion), of which 37 percent went to 22,104 insider hires, and the remaining 63 percent to 103,494 unionized employees. The one exception, Carlos Romero Deschamps,[77] earns a modest union salary on paper, but in reality makes as much as the managing director of Pemex.

*

The pensions received by ex-presidents and their families should also be eliminated. In this instance, it's not merely about making

---

77 A politician who appeared on *Forbes*'s 2013 list of "10 Most Corrupt Mexicans"; he is accused of using his status as leader of the oil workers union for private gain.

savings, but the abolishment of sinecures that ordinary Mexicans
rightly find outrageous. President Luis Echeverría[78] first implemented the practice of assigning armed forces personnel to protect
former presidents. From then on, with no justification, the following personnel have been assigned to them:

Accord 7637, November 25, 1976
Estimated cost in 2017 of personnel in service to ex-presidents
Pesos (Thousands of US dollars)

Army		(e)	
1	General	3,914,010 (215)	3,914,010 (215)
4	Lieutenant colonel	1,031,478 (57)	4,125,912 (226)
8	Lieutenant	541,659 (30)	4,333,272 (238)
32	Troops	289,054 (16)	9,249,728 (508)
Navy		(e)	
2	Commander	1,406,573 (77)	2,813,146 (154)
4	Frigate Lieutenant	606,089 (33)	2,424,356 (133)
16	Troops	327,263 (18)	5,236,208 (287)
Airforce		(e)	
1	Lieutenant colonel	1,031,478 (57)	1,031,478 (57)
2	Lieutenant	541,659 (30)	1,083,318 (59)
8	Troops	327,263 (18)	2,618,204 (144)
78	Total estimated		36,829,532 (2,021)

Source: Budget for the 2017 Fiscal Year, Volume IX "Analysis of Positions and Remunerations." 30% hazard pay was added.

78 Information regarding Accords 7637 and 2763-Bis were obtained by a request
for information Folio# 0210000053704 Dated October 21, 2004, requested by
a citizen to the then Federal Institute of Access to Public Information (IFAI).

ACCORD 2763-BIS, March 31, 1987
Estimated cost in 2017 of civil personnel in service to ex-presidents
Pesos (Thousands of US dollars)

Quantity	Personnel	Unitary	Total
1	Secretary of State	3,377,472 (185)	3,377,472 (185)
1	Life Insurance (e)	30,000 (2)	30,000 (2)
1	Major Medical Expense Insurance	25,000 (1)	25,000 (1)
	Pension levelled to that of secretary of State		3,432,472 (188)
78	Estimated total		36,829,532 (2,021)
	Civil Personnel (excludes extraordinary remuneration)	(e)	
1	General Director	3,185,215 (175)	3,185,215 (175)
2	Area Directors	1,602,965 (88)	3,205,930 (176)
4	Subdirectors	830,383 (46)	3,321,532 (182)
4	Department Heads	507,146 (28)	2,028,584 (111)
1	Secretariat of the General Director (e)	622,223 (34)	622,223 (34)
1	Secretariat of Area Director (e)	438,048 (24)	438,048 (24)
2	Secretariat of the Subdirector (e)	347,614 (19)	695,228 (38)
3	Specialized technicians (e)	228,190 (13)	684,570 (38)
3	Chauffeurs (e)	228,190 (13)	684,570 (38)
4	Auxiliary assistants (e)	161,078 (9)	644,312 (35)
4	Auxiliary assistants (e)	148,500 (8)	594,000 (33)
25			15,510,212 (851)
	Estimated total per ex-president		55,772,216 (3,061)

e) Estimated
Source: Budget for the 2016-2017 Fiscal Year, Volume IX "Analysis of Positions and Remunerations."

Subsequently, President Miguel de la Madrid issued Accord 2763-Bis, which added twenty-five civilian staff members to the already existing seventy-eight military positions, and a lifetime pension equivalent to the secretary of state's salary, with concomitant adjustments, as well as life insurance and major medical expenses.

Miguel de la Madrid's accord also introduced a pension for widows of ex-presidents of 80 percent of the secretary of state's salary during the first year following their death, which declines by 10 percent each year until leveling off at 50 percent. Widows, too, are provided with life insurance, and major medical costs are covered at 60 percent of what the office holder is entitled to.

Children of ex-presidents also have major medical expenses covered until they reach adulthood.

These expenses total some 244 million pesos (US$13.3 million), as the following chart details:

ESTIMATED GROSS COST OF THE ACCORDS
Pesos (Millions of US dollars)

	Estimated total cost per ex-president	(e)	228,119,331 (13)
1	Felipe Calderón		54,262,111 (3)
1	Vincent Fox		48,942,394 (3)
1	Ernesto Zedillo (only turned down the pension)		37,847,184 (2)
1	Carlos Salinas (only turned down the pension)		42,881,810 (2)
1	Luis Echeverría		44,185,832 (2)
	Estimated cost of two widows of ex-presidents	(e)	3,715,219 (0.2)
	60% of the Secretary of State's salary for Mrs. Paloma Delia Margarita Cordero Tapia		2,026,483 (0.1)
	50% of the Secretary of State's salary for Mrs. Alexandra Acimovic Popovic (Sasha Montenegro)		1,688,736 (0.1)
	Grand total		231,834,550 (13)

Source: National Institute for Transparency (INAI), Folio 0210000089216, Budget for the 2016 Fiscal Year, Volume IX "Analysis of Positions and Remunerations." 2016's numbers were amended with expected inflation of 1.0331, to reach 2017 numbers.

Ernesto Villanueva's book, *The Parasites of Power,* asserts that "in addition, ex-presidents enjoy a host of other benefits, including mobile phone services (including long distance calls); a vehicle for personal use, one for his wife, one for his kids, and three for his bodyguards; property taxes paid by the State; and car maintenance and upkeep. They also cover gardening services; electricity and cleaning; and bonuses."[79]

Luis Echeverría's retirement package was signed not by him but by the Defense and Navy secretaries, whereas Miguel de Madrid's was signed by the secretary for programming and budgeting. This is because, as per Article 89 of the Constitution, the president is not authorized to confer these benefits on ex-presidents. The rule of law was neatly skirted. It's interesting to note that none of these accords were published in the *Official Journal of the Federation,* yet no charges were filed as a result.

There is no legal or constitutional basis for these retirement packages, and we must do away with the unfair privileges they confer.

The Federal Expense Budget of 2017, Article 19, Section IV, Paragraph 4, establishes that "the Administrative Branch 02 Office of the Republic [...] includes the resources to cover this compensation for those who have left the charge of Chief Executive; or barring that, to whom they shall apply."

The following graph shows the sums that will be paid out in 2017 to ex-presidents and their widows, in line with the aforementioned accords. It's relevant to note that ex-presidents Carlos Salinas and Ernesto Zedillo supposedly relinquished their pensions, but not the remaining benefits, which far exceed the value of those pensions.

---

79 Ernesto Villanueva and Hilda Nucci, *The Parasites of Power: How Much Do the Mexican People Spend on the Benefits of Ex-Presidents?* (México: Ediciones Proceso, 2016).

ANNUAL ESTIMATED GROSS COST OF EX-PRESIDENTS PER THE ACCORDS AND QUERIES OF THE INAI

Pesos (Thousands of US dollars)

EX-PRESIDENT	Annual Salary	Civil Personnel	Military Personnel	Total
Widow of José López Portillo	1,688,736 (93)	-	-	1,688,736 (93)
Widow of Miguel de la Madrid	2,026,483 (111)	-	-	2,026,483 (111)
Luis Echeverría	3,432,472 (188)	3,923,828 (215)	36,829,532(2021)	44,185,832 (2,425)
Carlos Salinas	55,000 (3)	5,997,278 (329)	36,829,532(2021)	42,881,810 (2,353)
Ernesto Zedillo	55,000 (3)	962,652(53)	36,829,532(2021)	37,847,184 (2,077)
Vincent Fox	3,432,472 (188)	8,680,390 (476)	36,829,532(2021)	48,942,394 (2,686)
Felipe Calderón	3,432,472 (188)	14,000,107(768)	36,829,532(2021)	54,262,111 (2,978)
Total	14,122,635(775)	33,564,255(1,842)	184,147,660(10,106)	231,834,550 (12,723)

Source: National Institute for Transparency (INAI), Folio 0210000089216, Budget for the 2016 Fiscal Year, Volume IX "Analysis of Positions and Remunerations." 2016's numbers were amended with expected inflation of 1.0331, to reach 2017 numbers.

According to journalist Álvaro Delgado, on November 30, 2012, the last day of his term of office, Felipe Calderón reformed the Regulations of the Presidential Guard in order to retain the same number of guards in his service after leaving office, and to include the option to take on more should he so choose. Brazenly, he enacted the following order: "Ex-presidents shall maintain the same number of General Guards that they had assigned for security for themselves and their family; effective immediately. This notwithstanding required approval under Section IX of Article 11." Section IX asserts that the ex-president and his family can request yet more military protection if they choose to. In his last act before handing over power to Enrique Peña Nieto, Calderón modified regulations to guarantee free access to medical care at the Hospital Center of the Presidential Guard for himself and his family.

Furthermore, Calderón forced the Presidential Guard to "plan, organize, provide and manage all services to ensure the immediate safety of ex-presidents and their families, carrying out risk assessments where necessary in order to assign relevant security measures."[80]

The aforementioned article states that "Calderón already had 425 agents at his service." In other words, when this decree was implemented, the 103 personnel to which he was entitled under the previous accords mushroomed to 425. Total payroll costs for this staff of 425 people has never been released by the treasury. However, when one factors in both the explicitly provided benefits, as well as those expressed in the Regulations of the Presidential Guard, we estimate that in 2017 the expenditures associated with these benefits would rise to around 500 million pesos (US$27.2 million).

The entitled arrogance of these measures is perhaps best illustrated by comparing what our most recent ex-president costs the

---

80 Álvaro Delgado, *The secret Peña-Calderón pact: Story of an Affair* (México: Revista Proceso, 2016), 9.

treasury of Mexico, compared to what other former heads of state receive worldwide.

*

Consistent with the above, we should also adjust the operating expenses of the Federal Electricity Commission by taking a closer look at the "subsidies" received by the companies that sell them energy. This is a shady business; lucrative for transnational corporations but wildly costly for the treasury. Since the electricity industry began to be privatized in 1992, private enterprise has received a subsidy of 20 billion pesos (US$1 billion) per year. In 2017, of the 72.4 billion pesos (US$3.9 billion) that were budgeted for independent energy producers, 47.1 billion (US$2.5 billion) are to be invoiced for energy acquisition, which is privately produced. The remaining 25.2 billion (US$1.3 billion) (35 percent) were assigned as payment for services for so-called "fixed charges" for the capacity to generate energy. In contracts issued by the government with external producers, it has been established that the Federal Electricity Commission must charge an additional fee for operations and maintenance. That is to say, they hand over a subsidy of a kind that does not exist in the United States, Spain, or any place in the world where true competition and the free market prevails.

Mexican consumers are therefore hit with higher energy tariffs than American consumers.

We're aware that one must uphold contracts signed by previous authorities, but the majority of these documents were originally signed to be effective at a later date and, given that the rules of the game are changing, these ought to be reexamined. These profit margins explain the motivation for dismantling the Federal Electricity Committee's energy generation capabilities. The ruse of those who champion this is to disband a public enterprise so that the private sector can take over. Its dismantling is not part of a an efficiency drive or a search for economic savings, but simply a corrupt business arrangement.

*

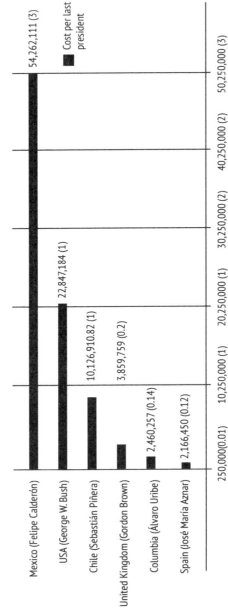

COST COMPARED TO PENSIONS RECIEVED BY EX-PRESIDENTS IN OTHER COUNTRIES
Pesos (Millions of US dollars)

Mexico (Felipe Calderón) — 54,262,111 (3)

USA (George W. Bush) — 22,847,184 (1)

Chile (Sebastián Piñera) — 10,126,910.82 (1)

United Kingdom (Gordon Brown) — 3,859,759 (0.2)

Columbia (Álvaro Uribe) — 2,460,257 (0.14)

Spain (José María Aznar) — 2,166,450 (0.12)

Cost per last president

250,000(0.01)   10,250,000 (1)   20,250,000 (1)   30,250,000 (2)   40,250,000 (2)   50,250,000 (3)

Note: The cost of Felipe Calderón's pension does not include the 2012 reforms nor the benefits covered by the Office of th Presidency. In terms of Spain, ex-president José Luis Rodríguez Zapatero was not selected because he took the role of Permanent Councillor of State, though he could later choose to charge his lifetime pension.
Source: https://www.fas.org/sgp/crs/misc/RL34631.pdf
http://www.senado.cl/appsenado/index.php?mo=transparencia&ac=informeTransparencia&tipo=10
http://www.elmundo.es/grafico/internacional/2016/11/10/5810859e5fdeac7558b461d.html
http://elpoliticon.com/cuanto-gana-en-pension-un-ex-presidente-de-colombia/
http://www.lainformacion.com/espana/que-hacen-y-cuanto-ganan-los-ex-presidentes-aznar-gonzalez-y-zapatero_5ezVbbUDWdJ4sCjHVi6xg2/

Millions of Pesos (Billions of US Dollars)

Total savings to reassign	362,000 (20)
Savings from Nonprogrammable Expenses - Interest	5,000 (0.3)
Savings on Programmable Expenses -Chapter 1000 of Personal Services -Acquisitions and Contracts -Operating costs -Transfers, assignations, subsidies, etc.	357,000 (20) 132,000 (7) 120,000 (7) 27,000 (1) 78,000 (4)

In sum, the savings in government spending through our Austerity Plan would be as above:

Just as the eradication of corruption will entail a peaceful social revolution, austerity will serve as a moral example, and austerity savings will serve as the principle means of financing development. For politicians with a conservative mindset, there is no possibility of expenditure reduction. By contrast, we assert that the rationalizing of public expenditures is a critical, and wholly achievable, objective. One great example of needless expenditure that could have been better used elsewhere is the Estela de Luz monument,[81] a frivolous project funded by Calderón's administration that cost over 753 million pesos (US$41 million). When completed, the monument cost 192 percent more than was initially budgeted, and was completed sixteen months later than promised.[82] Similarly, the public works projects funded under Peña Nieto's administration ended up costing double what was originally quoted.

If we can rid ourselves of corruption and eliminate needless government spending, we'll save enough capital to finance development. This is the central tenet of our program regarding public

81 A public monument in Mexico City built in 2011 commemorating the bicentenary of Mexico's independence.

82 Auditoría Superior de la Federación. Informe del Resultado de la Fiscalización Superior de la Cuenta Pública 2011. Auditoría de Inversiones Físicas: 11–0-11J00–04-0056.

administration. It's possible to invest in the people without falling into debt. And I repeat emphatically: it's untrue that there are insufficient funds. Reassigning misallocated funds to the benefit of production, employment, and general well-being is a wholly attainable goal.

¡Oye, Trump! Speech 9
The US Government, Jekyll and Hyde

San Francisco, California, March 20, 2017

We've come here to express our support and solidarity with the Mexican people and with migrants who suffer persecution and discrimination. But the aim of this visit is also to raise awareness among conservative voters in the United States that their misfortunes were not caused by foreigners, despite what right-wing political rhetoric would have you believe.

In these times, as government propaganda pits us against one another and irresponsibly exploits jingoism, chauvinism, and hate, our task is to show that economic and social problems, in the US and around the world, are almost always caused by political corruption, impunity, factional interests, and the unequal distribution of wealth and income.

The US is a clear example of the truth that material wealth alone does not necessarily create better living or working conditions. The US has, by far, the largest economy in the world. However, in the quality of life index of 2016, the US sits at 13th place, below Ireland, Switzerland, Norway, Luxemburg, Sweden, Australia, Iceland, Italy, Denmark, Spain, Singapore, and Finland.

As for the thirty cities with the greatest quality of life, eighteen of them are in Europe, six in Oceania, four in Canada, one in Asia, and only one (San Francisco) in the US.

It's clear that this country faces very significant social problems. This is plainly revealed by the fact that there are 45 million poor people residing in the US, nearly 15 percent of the population.

It is regrettable that instead of taking action to reduce poverty and inequality, the US government blames Mexico and the Mexican people for its problems. Instead of building walls, and persecuting migrants, it would be more humane and efficient to implement good governance and work toward the well-being of all.

Instead of blaming others, US elites should recognize that something is wrong when a huge economic and technological power like the US offers a lower quality of life than many poorer countries and when tens of millions of its own citizens live beneath the poverty line.

A few statistics: The US occupies thirty-sixth place in terms of worldwide poverty; and it is number eighteen in terms of corruption. It is one of the most unequal societies in the world. According to the Organisation for Economic Cooperation and Development (OECD), the average salary in the US is lower than in Luxembourg, Holland, Australia, Belgium, Germany, France, New Zealand, Ireland, the United Kingdom, Canada, and Japan. The World Economic Forum places the US sixteenth in quality of education, and the UN puts it at twenty-eighth place in terms of health.

Furthermore, the US has a highly regressive taxation system. Proportionally speaking, workers contribute more than large corporations, and many business tycoons are able to evade paying taxes. The US loses out on $337 billion per year due to tax evasion.

Arms spending by the US government dwarfs spending in other countries. Washington's defense budget is $522 billion per year, which exceeds the *combined* spending of China, Russia, Saudi Arabia, the United Kingdom, France, Germany, Japan, India, and Israel, according to the International Institute for Strategic Studies.

Recently Donald Trump proposed to Congress a military budget of $574 billion—that is to say, a 10 percent increase—while government investment in housing is reduced by 14 percent, transportation by 13 percent, education by 14 percent, health by 16 percent, justice by 20 percent, agriculture by 21 percent, development programs by 29 percent, and environmental protection by 31 percent.

This explains to a large degree why there is a greater quality of life in Ireland, Norway, Sweden, Iceland, Denmark, Italy, and Spain. The poorly managed American public health system has taken a severe toll on the American people. Moreover, unlike many countries, the US does not offer free public education beyond high school.

Why, instead of blaming migrants, don't politicians speak honestly? Why don't they change economic policy to prioritize the material and spiritual needs of the people of this great nation?

The very history of San Francisco demonstrates the extent to which transformative social change is possible in pursuit of a better world.

It's no coincidence that this is the only US city that is included among the thirty cities with the highest quality of life in the world. Significantly, the city owes its very name to Saint Francis of Assisi, the deacon who rejected material goods and dedicated his life to finding happiness through serving others.

Yet even though San Francisco is a city of brotherhood, a true sanctuary of liberty and tolerance, we must continue to raise awareness among those who have been manipulated by the campaign that seeks to stigmatize Mexicans and other migrants. Let's work toward a world without discrimination or borders, where justice, peace, and solidarity reign supreme.

In terms of well-being, we should think not only of the satisfaction of material needs but also of the strengthening of social, moral, and spiritual principles.

Of course, no one can achieve well-being without access to work, food, housing, and health services. Those in poverty must first focus on survival before attending to political, scientific, artistic, or spiritual pursuits.

But the meaning of life must not be reduced to obtaining material wealth. "Man does not live by bread alone," as the saying goes, and an individual without a code of morals does not necessarily achieve happiness. In some cases, wealth gained through unscrupulous practices leads to an empty and dehumanized life. One must always seek the balance between spiritual and material needs, ensuring that people have all they need to thrive and to cultivate their best qualities.

I am sure that the problems that plague Mexico and the US could be resolved were the governments of both nations to commit to overcoming inequality, poverty, and corruption in their respective territories. Sooner rather than later, we would then see the flourishing of an era of liberty and fellowship on both sides of the border.

CHAPTER 9

A BLUEPRINT FOR MEXICO'S ECONOMIC AND SOCIAL REVITALIZATION

Freeing up funds for development by rationalizing the budget will allow us to maintain macroeconomic equilibrium and avoid financial crises. Our program centers on managing debt and inflation and investing in employment and well-being. But development, contrary to the claims and policies of neoliberal technocrats, depends not only on a monetary policy of controlling inflation and fiscal discipline, but also on fostering economic growth to improve living and working conditions.

We call for a disciplined approach to the handling of macroeconomic variables. We emphasize the importance of combating economic stagnation, but growth must be accompanied by an equitable distribution of its benefits and, I would add, a generous, humanist mode of thinking. GDP growth alone is not enough: the benefits of development must reach everyone. We must progress in a just way, for progressing unjustly is no progress at all. We strive toward modernity—but a modernity forged from below, for and with everyone.

In our view, the state is an engine of development. Unlike those who expect the market to correct itself, we believe that public intervention is essential to reactivate the economy and to create jobs, above all in periods of recession, such as the one we currently face in Mexico.

The government has the tools at its disposal to foster cooperation among the public, private, and social sectors for the well-being of all. Collaboration of this nature is essential for building a strong economy and a just society; all of our contributions are indispensable in achieving progress with equity.

We have seen that it is possible. In Mexico City, the rehabilitation of the Reforma-Centro corridor was achieved through the cooperation of the private sector, civil society, and the federal and city governments. The historic Reforma Avenue was renovated, a project that had not been undertaken since 1968. This in turn gave life to the Alameda zone, which had been left in ruins since the earthquakes of 1985, and thirty-seven blocks of the historic center were restored.

The government of Mexico City invested 675 million pesos (US$36.8 million) in this program. The private sector developed 195 construction and remodeling projects, investing 16 billion pesos (US$872 million). That is to say, each peso of public investment drew 23.3 pesos (US$1.27) in private investment. This initiative was so successful because trust was fostered, bureaucracy was simplified, and fiscal stimuli were provided. Through our joint efforts, we improved our infrastructure and beautified the city. This will be our modus operandi if we win the presidency in 2018. Through seed funding, we will attract private investment and create jobs.

The convergence of public and private investment will be supported through regional development strategies. We have studied each region in order to define each region's economic needs. With a focus on sustainable development, we will create programs that take advantage of natural resources, technology, and public-private sphere cooperation, always with the active participation of the public. Development policies (in agriculture, manufacturing, tourism, infrastructure, and other sectors) must always consider the regional context; they must see the populace as active participants in the design and execution of the programs they pursue.

A central priority for the new government will be the development of the southeast, which for centuries has suffered the paradox of being rich in resources (petroleum, gas, water, biodiversity, cultural heritage, tourist potential), but whose population lives in poverty due to inadequate distribution of wealth. It's time to reinvigorate the region through a development plan centered on the prudent use of gas and petroleum; the modernization of hydroelectric plants in the Grijalva and Papalopan rivers; reforestation; strengthening of the agribusiness sector; the construction of refineries, ports, railways, highways; and investment in social development.

We will work transparently, with well-defined strategies, priorities, and goals. The state must inspire hope, but not at the cost of resorting to false promises and demagoguery. We must accurately estimate the cost of programs and their economic and social viability. We shall concentrate resources, time, and talent on projects that will bring about the greatest degree of collective well-being. We shall abide by the popular saying "Do few things, if you must, but do them well." A few examples:

1. Investment in the countryside: recognizing its social, environmental, and cultural contributions toward food sovereignty

Our plan for growth with justice is not viable without providing support to the long-neglected countryside and its inhabitants. We shall promote rural development by improving the living conditions of agricultural workers and by working to increase productivity.

There are 5.8 million rural households in Mexico (INEGI, ENIGH 2002) in 180,000 localities of 2,500 or fewer inhabitants (Population and Housing Census, 2010). Rural dwellers represent 21 percent of the national population—some 25 million people (INEGI 2015). Five million agricultural workers—*ejido* members, communalists, and small landowners—possess 90 percent of the nation's territory. This land is not merely agricultural, but contains a wealth of resources, minerals, natural wonders, and historic and cultural assets. These resources are invaluable if we look beyond mere monetary wealth. Supporting the countryside entails strengthening our greatest cultural assets.

The countryside generates huge environmental benefits for the population and the economy: water, clean air, reduction of greenhouse gases, climatic regulation, preservation of biodiversity, conservation, and regeneration of forests, among others.

First, we must support our people by eradicating poverty, improving the living conditions in settlements, *ejidos*, communities, and towns, and slowing the flow of migration from the countryside to the cities. As we've said, the countryside is crucial to the health of our environment, but it is also a resource for development.

A strong agricultural sector would confer many advantages: increased availability of foodstuffs and raw materials to meet internal demand and support economic stability; the export of profitable crops; the generation of agricultural jobs to reduce flight to the cities; all of these benefits would cascade across the broader economy.

Supporting agricultural production requires, in my opinion, a profound change in policy. Above all, we must abandon the neoliberal notion that the value of the countryside can only be counted in its monetary worth. And we must also reject the neoliberal belief that agricultural workers must resignedly accept whatever brutal conditions are imposed by the market.

This erroneous belief arises from the flawed premise that by giving private actors complete freedom, spontaneous market forces will increase capital investment in the agricultural sector and increase efficiency and production of foodstuffs and raw materials. Following our adoption of NAFTA, this program was aggressively pursued.

Through this neoliberal vision, technocrats embraced open trade without strategic limits, which left domestic producers at a marked disadvantage. NAFTA favored US producers, who are able to sell below market prices due to advanced technology and generous government subsidies. Mexican farmers do not receive these protections, and are left largely to fend for themselves.

The damaging effects of the opening of the Mexican agricultural economy to US producers were aggravated through sharp cuts in public agricultural investment. Between 1980–82, this public investment comprised 1.48 percent of GDP. From 2001–03, this number dropped to 0.68 percent . By 2011–13, it had collapsed to just to 0.08 percent.

Public agricultural spending worldwide during the same period fell from 2.93 percent to 0.58 percent of GDP. Between 2011–13, it had fallen to 0.46 percent of GDP.

This period saw cuts to research and development across the agricultural, forestry, and fishery sectors. Even as the Organisation for Economic Co-operation and Development (OECD) recommended research and development spending of at least 1 percent of GDP (developed countries already spend around 3 percent), Mexico allocated a mere 0.42 percent in 2003, of which 0.03 percent went to agricultural, forestry, and fishery research. Research centers dedicated to agricultural and fishery studies are long-abandoned.

Rural people have been abandoned in every sense of the word. The actual land under cultivation that was supported by Bank of Development financing dropped from 16,217,526 acres per year from 1980–82, to a mere 3,518,780 acres per year between 2001–03. By 2011–13, it fell to 3,138,238 acres per year. According to the National Agricultural Survey of 2012 (INEGI), only 7.7 percent of production facilities were supported through bank financing.

The following graph demonstrates just how sharply agricultural, forestry, and fishery loans have fallen in the past twenty years from both commercial and development banks.

CREDIT TO THE AGRIBUSINESS, FORESTRY AND FISHERY SECTORS AS A PERCENTAGE OF OVERALL CREDIT

— Commercial Bank

Source: INEGI (Several years). The Food System in Mexico. Mexico. Federal Government (2016). Fourth Briefing of Enrique Peña Nieto. Mexico.

What's more, the system of guaranteed prices, implemented under General Lázaro Cárdenas, was eliminated by the neoliberal technocrats under the pretext that it was an outdated agricultural practice, when in truth Salinas's government had committed to it upon agreeing to NAFTA. However, this system is employed to great effect worldwide to provide a level of price certainty for agricultural producers. For example, in the United States, the 2002–07 Farm Bill established a "target income" to guarantee the prices of corn, soy, rice, sorghum, and other products.

The result of neoliberal policies being applied to our rural areas is a grave lag in growth of the agricultural sector compared to population growth. From 1980–83 to 2001–03, agricultural, forestry, and fishery GDP per inhabitant went down by 11.1 percent. In other words, while overall production of food advanced at an annual increase of 1.4 percent, during the same period the national population grew at a rate of 1.9 percent per year.

The most severely affected food groups are the major grains (corn, beans, wheat, rice, soy, sorghum, safflower, and sesame), whose harvest diminished from 341.2 kilograms per inhabitant to 304.5 kilograms—a reduction of 10.8 percent.

Production of red meat went from 36.5 kilograms per inhabitant to 25.5 kilograms, a reduction of 30.2 percent; milk production fell from 103.9 liters per inhabitant to 95.8 liters, a reduction of 7.9 percent; and the production of timber went down from 131.6 cubic decimeters per habitant to 73.2 cubic decimeters, a 44.2 percent fall.

In contrast, agricultural food imports rose from $2.76 billion per year from 1980–82, to $5.56 billion from 1991–93, just before the implementation of NAFTA, to $11.88 billion per year in 2001–03, to $27.4 billion per year from 2011–13. It's worth noting that in 2003, $12.8 billion were spent on these imports, exceeding the sum total of foreign direct investment, which was $10.7 billion that year.

It's true that our agricultural exports have grown, but at the cost of neglecting our internal market; indeed, exports have not offset the growing imports of foodstuffs and raw materials. The deficit in the commercial balance in foodstuffs went from $694 million per year in the period from 1980–82, to $3 billion per year in 2001–03, to $4.3 billion in 2011–13.

Since NAFTA's implementation in 1994, all the way through to 2015, total food imports have reached $357 billion; each year we've lost $16.25 billion buying food that we could be producing ourselves. The total sum of the trade imbalance throughout NAFTA's lifetime has grown to $60.7 billion, with an average annual deficit of $2.76 billion.

One must recall that for each dollar spent on importing food, Mexico not only spends precious foreign currency that could be put toward more productive ends, but also loses rural jobs by lowering wages for agricultural workers and aggravating rural poverty. We lose, too, the exponential effects of agricultural activity on production, jobs, and related investment across the economy.

Many jobs have been lost because of a lack of agricultural investment. In 1993, 8,842,774 people were employed in the agricultural sector. By 2003, that number fell to 6,813,644, a loss of 2 million jobs during that short period. By 2016, the population working in the agricultural sector fell to 6,615,476, as workers left en masse for the cities and abroad.

Our abandonment of rural areas has left these workers with little choice. Millions of Mexicans, by necessity, have had to leave their native lands.

According to the National Population Council, during the first three years of Vicente Fox's term, the flow of Mexican migrants to the United States grew to a historically high level of 410,000 people per year.

Mexico now exports more migrant labor than any country on earth. This socioeconomic phenomenon has broken strong cultural ties among indigenous and peasant communities. Previously, immigration was largely confined to the northern and central states. Now, peasant workers from states like Veracruz, Chiapas and Tabasco, especially the young, are opting to migrate. In many communities, only women, children, and the elderly have stayed behind.

Net migration flow (arrivals minus departures) by period

Period	Flow in period	Average per year	Source
1960 - 1970	290 000	29 000	1
1970 - 1980	1 550 000	155 000	1
1980 - 1990	2 600 000	260 000	1
1990 - 1995	1 575 000	315 000	1
1996 - 1999	1 182 000	295 000	2
2000 - 2003	1 230 000	410 000	3
2005 - 2010	1 814 000	302 000	2

1 SRE. Mexico-US Study. Mexico, 1997.
2 CONAPO estimates.
3 Milenio Semanal estimate based on CONAPO's most recent dates.

Despite the fact that Mexico is rich in natural resources, and despite the profound love that our people have for our country, these hard-working people have had few options. One only need consider the wealth of indigenous and peasant knowledge that has been passed down for generations. This knowledge has been undervalued and disdained throughout the neoliberal period. Those who manage economic policy have never concerned themselves with the countryside. Pedro Aspe's[83] words weigh heavy: "In a globalized world, there will be no need to invest in the agricultural sector, since we can get everything from abroad, for cheaper." This simplistic and irresponsible mode of thinking is not without consequence: the abandonment of our rural areas has taken a heavy toll on production, has increased migration, and fostered societal breakdown and violence. Unbelievable though it seems, some functionaries still prefer to let migration rates rise than to invest in rural development. They instead push for training programs in landscaping, nursing, and elderly home care in the expectation that these workers will be employed in the United States as the US population ages.

Clearly, to accept this argument is to surrender our own capacity for sovereign development. Reversing the decades of neglect of

83   Secretary of finance under Salinas.

our rural areas will be no easy task; poverty, at this point, is deeply entrenched. However, we believe that through swift and efficient government investment in our rural areas and its people, we can reverse the devastation and work toward growth and well-being.

We therefore propose to implement the following measures immediately:

A) A comprehensive agricultural development program across the countryside. We must harmonize and support production with an aim toward self-sufficiency, increasing internal demand and exports. We will fast track a program of targeted support for small producers who account for 85 percent of domestic production. We will stop neglecting them, and show that we recognize their great potential.

A policy that includes agricultural exports does not preclude one that satisfies internal demand. Both are possible and have coexisted in our past. Our history shows as much: from 1940–60, agricultural exports comprised more than half of export revenues; in the same period, our rural areas satisfied internal demand of raw materials and foodstuffs.

B) We will promote economic self-sufficiency among communities. We will foster traditional productive activities through small investments. Rescuing our rural areas entails revaluing the productive capabilities of our people. These capabilities have nurtured and sustained our people for generations.

Cultivation for self-consumption, which millions of indigenous people and agricultural workers rely on, has allowed for the conservation of an invaluable diversity of species and native maize crops that make up Mexico's genetic and biocultural wealth. These species must thrive, and we therefore oppose genetically modified corn.

We must support the use of traditional crops and technologies that have been consigned to oblivion due to a neoliberal conception of modernity. Traditional agriculture can be a valuable source of income in rural communities.

There are still parts of Mexico where indigenous communities continue to produce all that they consume. Historically, in *pueblos* like Tlaxcala, peasants harvest maize on small, productive plots of land, and keep goats, sheep, and cows on their patios.

Instead of supporting these activities, large poultry and pig farms have been constructed, with "purebred" animals that are less resistant to disease and depend on special meal from foreign firms, providing little benefit to the farmworkers themselves.

It's regrettable that in some communities, peasants have to buy hens and eggs, when they themselves could produce and sell these foods.

We propose creating lines of credit for the purchase of animals, grains, seeds, and equipment to support productive and traditional agricultural practices, enriched through a dialogue between indigenous knowledge and modern scientific and technological advances.

We must improve the economic status of our agricultural workers. To this end, we will organize a national crusade in support of our rural areas, putting over 20,000 unemployed or under-utilized farm workers to work, whilst respecting cultural traditions and the agricultural conditions on the ground.

These activities will yield improvements in nutrition, income, self-sufficiency, well-being, and a strengthening of cultural identity.

It won't suffice to create urban jobs. The absorption of the rural population by other sectors of the economy would require unrealistic growth rates of over 10 percent per year. We therefore must bring efficient production practices to the countryside, and, simultaneously, we must support subsistence farming, which allows workers to provide for their families.

C) To support production for the internal market, it's necessary to implement a new system that guarantees prices to agricultural producers. We must establish a system of price guarantees—or "objective income,"introduced to Mexico through peasant movements in 2003—throughout our neglected rural areas. The system of guaranteed prices or income would cover all basic grains (maize, beans, wheat, and rice), basic oilseeds and textile fibers (cotton, soy, safflower, and sesame), as well as sorghum and barley. This new system would make the government the buyer of last resort, and be coupled with the construction of strategic nutritional reserves. This would be a long-term project, with a horizon of ten years.

This project would allow us to provide certainty to agricultural producers, correcting the discriminatory nature of our current system of subsidies that excludes most small producers. We will extend support to subsistence farm workers who sell their excess produce to the market for knock-down prices.

We estimate that through these policies, we will achieve self-sufficiency within three years in basic foods, such as maize, beans, rice, sorghum, wheat, beef, pork, poultry, and fish.

D) It's essential to support high-density agricultural exports. For decades now, Mexico has made a name for itself on the global stage exporting coffee, avocados, tomatoes, melons, mangos, and numerous other horticultural products. We will pursue a strategic program to rescue the coffee industry, which faces crisis through governmental neglect. We must invest in technology, climate, and quality control, and support the overseas commercial promotion of these products.

E) As for currently extant government programs, such as Proagro (previously Procampo) and others, we propose to transform these programs into real instruments for change. We will counter the hoarding of subsidies by a small handful of large agricultural firms. These resources will be disbursed at the federal level, to ensure an equitable distribution of support to all regions.

F) We must invest in rural infrastructure to maximize our use of irrigated land: optimizing water use in these districts, rebuilding rural streets and highways, expanding research centers, and refurbishing and expanding rural warehouses. Benefits to the agricultural sector aside, these investments will generate construction jobs and will contribute to growth on a national scale.

We must increase credit availability to the agricultural sector through the National Development Bank as well as commercial banks through rediscounts through Trust Funds for Rural Development (FIRA). Additionally, we will support the development of new financial intermediaries in the rural sphere that will promote the self-organization of producers. Meanwhile, we must strengthen and expand our agricultural capacity, while ensuring financial support is not concentrated on just a few large firms.

In the southeast, we will pursue two strategies to redevelop large tracts of unproductive land. The first is to make use of pastures that have been delegated to secondary vegetation through the abandonment of livestock. The rescue of neglected pastures will be accompanied by the granting of new credit lines. We will import 2 million heifers over the course of three years. Our second strategy consists of expanding the surface area dedicated to crops like bananas, cacao, citrus, and fruits with the aim of building agro-industrial associations modeled on the Pascual Cooperative.

Meanwhile, we will plant 2,471,053 acres of trees for timber. Deforestation has taken a massive toll, destroying the tropical rainforest in the absence of government protection or rational management. Thus, we will prioritize the protection of forestry activity. One such project is sowing cedars and mahogany trees in the Huastecas (Tamaulipas, San Luis Potosí, Hidalgo, and Veracruz) and across the southeast. This will generate 400,000 jobs per year, anchor young agricultural workers to nature, stem the migration flow, reforest and rescue native flora and fauna, and allow us to reach self-sufficiency in the production of timber (we currently import 50 percent of that which we consume). We're aware that this is a project that will yield its greatest benefits over the course of time, but we must start it now as its economic, ecologic, and social importance is enormous.

To ensure the financing of these development projects, we will increase the agricultural budget by at least 50 billion pesos (US$2.7 billion) per year, and we expect to maintain it at this level, in real terms, until 2024.

G) We must prioritize scientific research if our rural areas are to thrive. We must invest in agricultural research centers across the country—the National Institute of Forestry, Agriculture, and Livestock Research (INIFAP), the Center for Investigation and Advanced Studies (Cinvestav), and others, in tandem with agricultural universities, in the search for new technologies. Innovation in this field will be fostered through financial incentives and an efficient system of rural and forestry development.

The integration of research centers with rural areas will be implemented swiftly. Toward that end, we will enlist the help of passionate and talented researchers who have devoted their lives to applying science for the benefit of our nation.

It's crucial to prevent further mismanagement of the rural environment. We will fight for the conservation and restoration of our environment, working toward a sustainable food system that reconciles humans with nature; we will promote the protection of biodiversity, especially the flora and fauna at risk of extinction; and we will incentivize carefully implemented natural resource and environmental development.

Toward this end, it is essential to support organic horticulture and to restrict the use of pesticides whenever possible.

One important element of our plan for agricultural development and environmental protection is a new working policy for the collection, management, and distribution of water. As part of that new policy, we will support the fishing industry with an eye toward conservation and sustainability. Mexico possesses some 235,000 square kilometers of bodies of water (rivers, lakes, arroyos, dams); 11,200 square kilometers of coastal waters; and 3,160,000 square kilometers of territorial sea; resources that can be used optimally and responsibly to generate economic growth, improve the nutrition of our people, create jobs, and improve the living conditions of coastal communities nationwide.

H) NAFTA member countries must pursue cooperative agreements to overcome existing technological, subsidy, and productivity-related asymmetries. Independent of these negotiations, we must make strategic use of tariffs and other safeguards to ensure that Mexico can protect its producers and avoid the predatory practices so common in international trade.

This vision is not nostalgic, nor does it yearn for a return to patronage. It's a demand to establish a new model of development that will fight for our rural areas and their citizens, and which will value them as important contributors to our economy and guarantors of nutritional self-sufficiency and job security. It is a demand for a new model of development that practices solidarity and inclusivity while protecting our natural resources and biodiversity.

In short, we shall rescue our rural areas from the neglect they have suffered under the neoliberal experiment. We will support domestic producers through subsidies and lines of credit to achieve food sovereignty. We will thereby tie the people to their communities, generating rural employment that will help stem the flow of migration.

2. Restore the energy sector and its potential

Even amid the great challenges we face stemming from the so-called energy reforms (the privatization of petroleum and electricity industries), we cannot and must not abandon this sector as a strategic resource for Mexico's sovereign development. It offers profitable opportunities at all stages of production, from the extraction of crude oil and gas to refinery, petrochemistry, and the generation of electricity. The products from these industries are inputs for others, and therefore form parts of larger value chains.

For example, the cement and steel industries require huge inputs of energy whose high import tariffs render the final product more expensive. In other instances, a consistent source of supply is vital to promote the development of certain industries, as many of these inputs are complex to transport and thus are not commercially viable for export to external markets. What's more, the electric energy industry purchases massive amounts of goods and services, which could potentially strengthen the domestic market. No modern economic activity can continue or remain competitive without the steady supply of electricity. It is projected that not only will demand increase but that by 2024 it will have doubled. Even as research continues into other sources of energy, the global economy will continue to rely on hydrocarbons as an energy source for many decades to come.

Here, Mexico has a distinct competitive advantage. Not having to rely on petroleum imports is a great thing indeed. Even while, during the neoliberal period, Mexico dropped from sixth to thirteenth among the largest exporters of petroleum worldwide, we have enough potential crude reserves to produce gasoline and petrochemicals. What's more, we have a wealth of natural gas used to generate electricity.

We will conduct a referendum on ownership of the energy sector. If we win the referendum we will bring the petroleum and electric industries back under public ownership. In addition, we must take urgent action, within the existing legal framework, to deal with the chronic inefficiencies of power generation overseen by the FEC. We must stop private corporations from exploiting these subsidies and thereby reduce our purchases of these resources from abroad.

Pemex's management has been characterized by theft and irrationality. We must free it from corruption. Pemex cannot continue to grant contracts worth millions of dollars to foreign firms and corrupt politicians. We must also end the practice of exporting our energy resources without replenishing reserves. From 2004 to the present, we went from producing 3,400,000 barrels to 2,247,000 barrels per day, and it is estimated that in 2018 production will drop to 1,900,000 barrels per day. This speaks to the disastrous effects of privatization. We are barely extracting enough to meet internal demand, and yet, because refineries and petrochemical plants were abandoned, we continue to sell crude oil and depend entirely on the import of gasoline and other derivatives.

We need a radical change in petroleum policy. We must take over the management of Pemex, invest in exploration, and begin construction of two large refineries in Dos Bocas, Tabasco, and Atasta, Campeche (both of which are located in close proximity to drilling sites. These projects will not only create jobs but allow us to cease importing 635,000 barrels of gasoline and diesel per day, or 60 percent of our internal consumption, at a cost of $25 billion per year. We are fully capable of processing our own raw materials, and we need not sell a single barrel more abroad. We must rescue the petrochemicals industry and support gasoline production in order to halt our rapid and growing dependence on external suppliers.

The Federal Electricity Commission's plants must operate at full capacity with the goal of reducing our purchases, at currently exorbitant prices, of electric energy from companies who through subsidies and overpriced sales have extracted nearly 60 billion pesos from the public budget.

In short, our plan is to integrate and modernize the electric energy industry, to create jobs, and to reduce energy prices for the benefit of consumers and small business owners. Of course, we are committed to supporting the development of renewable energy, so as not to squander the natural resources that later generations will inherit. Enacting this program will require an additional investment of 80 billion pesos (US$4.3 billion) per year.

3. Supporting growth and job creation

Modernizing the energy sector, a basic precondition for Mexico's successful industrialization and independent development, will require reforms and public works projects that will take time, but we can expect to see results within three years, once the new refineries are operating. While we move toward steady growth through this profound change, we must stimulate the economy in the short term to combat stagnation and to create jobs.

The failure of the neoliberal model is evidenced by our lack of economic growth: in thirty-one years, from 1984–2015, average GDP has grown by only 2 percent. If we consider population growth, per capita GDP grew by a mere 0.3 percent, according to the World Bank. The ideology imposed for the past two decades, which fails to consider the question of income distribution, has not been efficient even in quantitative terms. In the neoliberal period, growth has been virtually nil, with benefits accruing solely to wealthy elites. Our new projects, which will be geared toward stimulating the economy and creating jobs, will require an additional investment of 220 billion pesos (US$12 billion) for housing, public works, outreach, small business assistance, tourism, salaries, and the strengthening of consumption and the internal market. Our plans are as follows:

A) Support the construction industry

We have access to raw materials, necessary equipment, and expert civil engineers. Our construction workers are among the best in the world, and we are home to many important construction firms.

What's more, supporting this industry will lead to a variety of additional benefits: the economy will be revitalized, our infrastructure and public works will be improved, and jobs will be created. Through meaningful public-private-social sector collaboration, our infrastructure will be transformed. That transformation will see the building of new highways, high speed trains, airports, ports, dams, water and drainage systems, and schools, hospitals, and housing.

Specifically, we call for the implementation of the following projects:

- An urban and rural housing development project, with an annual goal of 500,000 new jobs created. Housing is a social good. Good quality housing fosters safety, a sense of stability, and local identity. This program will also spur economic activity, as it will involve at least 37 industrial and service industry sectors, translating into jobs both directly and indirectly; it will take the fullest advantage of our resources; and the economic activity of the project will promote regional development.

- A public works and services program (centering on the construction of potable water systems, drainage systems, nurseries, schools, hospitals, and recreation spaces) in populous neighborhoods in the Valley of Mexico, in border cities, and in the nation's periphery.

- The construction of new highways, especially in the southeast, that will serve the 362 municipalities (15 percent of all municipalities) that don't have paved roads. The construction of these roads will employ workers from the community to strengthen the local economy.

- The construction of two new runways at the Santa Lucía airbase to address the insufficient capacity of Mexico City's airports. By canceling the construction of the proposed Lake Texcoco airport, a costly and technically unsound project that exists only due to special interests and corruption, we will save over 100 billion pesos (US$5.4 billion).

- Creation of an economic corridor in Istmo de Tehuantepec.
  By uniting the Pacific with the Atlantic and facilitating the
  transport of goods between Asia and the East Coast, we
  can take advantage of our strategic location. We will build
  a cargo line along the 300-kilometer corridor, expand the
  existing highway, and refurbish the ports of Salina Cruz
  and Coatzacoalcos. We will take advantage of the region's
  petroleum, gas, water, wind, and electric power, and install
  assembly and manufacturing plants. This region will be a
  duty-free zone.

This project will be implemented through public-private-social
partnerships. Environmental safeguards and the rights of existing
tenants will be respected throughout the process. In particular,
landowners affected by the economic corridor's construction will
be invited to the table as shareholders of the new company created
to oversee the corridor's creation. The construction of new public
works and factories in the corridor will create jobs that will stem
the flow of immigration.

- The construction of a high speed train line from Mexico
  City to the US border, as well as a train line for those seek-
  ing culture along the Mayan route between Cancún and
  Palenque.

B) Supporting small and medium-sized businesses

State policy will promote development of small and medium-sized
businesses through the extension of cheap credit and protections
against unreasonable input prices, high taxes, and bureaucratic
costs. Let's not forget that small and medium-sized businesses are
responsible for 90 percent of existing jobs.

We must promote the creativity and productivity of the
Mexican people. Across the nation, small workshops and family
businesses make a wide variety of products with no governmental support whatsoever. The ingenuity of indigenous women who
create intricate embroideries and tapestries never ceases to amaze

me. The same can be said of the artisans of Olinalá, in Guerrero, or Zacoalco, in Jalisco, the carpenters in Huasteca—and many others who create products that are true works of art.

Prehispanic modes of commerce continue to flourish in Mexico. In the weekly markets in Oaxaca, Puebla, and Michoacán, people still barter, as they do in the great open air markets in San Martín Texmelucan, Puebla; Chiconcuac and San Mateo Atenco, in the State of Mexico. Let's not forget that it's thanks to this entrepreneurial spirit that people have overcome widespread economic adversity in the neoliberal age. Were it not for the informal economy and mass migration, we would have faced massive social unrest.

From our point of view, the best argument for job creation through the support of small businesses was articulated by Gabriel Zaid in an April 2011 article for *Reforma*. He argued that, amid such a shortage of jobs, we can't just focus on large firms:

Capital intensive investments increase labor's productivity rendering us competitive on a transnational scale. For that reason, they can't be the solution to low employment. Producing more with less people renders those people more productive, but does nothing for those unemployed. Expansion's *annual figures on Mexico's 500 largest companies make it clear that large investments can improve productivity without increasing personnel.*

Countries with surplus capital but a shortage of labor (to the point where they must import workers) develop technologies that enable production with fewer workers. Nations lacking in capital, but with a surplus of people (and consequent high levels of emigration) need technology that enables greater production without large capital inputs. In both cases, productivity increases, but through distinct approaches that respond to different situations.

Large infusions of capital to increase productivity by 20 or 30% is fine for economies that have already reached a high level of productivity. But using small infusions to increase productivity by 200% or 300% at a lower level of productivity is better: it makes the most of available capital.

Smaller targeted capital investments are not made because they lack the "sexiness" of large investment projects. Mexico's economic elite is proud (with good reason) that each day more Mexicans demonstrate that they are equal to or better than their international counterparts. But they are slower to realize that Mexico has to follow the same path of development as these now wealthy countries: they began as high-production economies with low levels of capital inputs, and only later achieved high productivity with fewer personnel.

Refusing to implement intermediate developmental policies and, in effect, trying to start at the finish line has led to the mass migration of Mexico's poor. Our economic policies have focused on the summit, not on the base of the pyramid. Consequently, the Mexican government has created millions of jobs for Mexico's poor . . . in the United States.

We propose turning the Ministry of Economy into a small business development unit, committing 10 billion additional pesos per year to the task. When I served as mayor of Mexico City, we created a new credit line for small businesses. From 2001–05, we invested 731 million pesos (US$39.8 million). Promisingly, 90 percent of borrowers honored their commitments and benefited greatly from the program.

C) Promote the tourism industry

Despite meager governmental support, the tourism sector has grown more than any other in recent years. It's common to hear those in the tourist industry of Quintana Roo speak of how they managed to put Cancún "on the map." This great accomplishment should be replicated across the country. Our country has a wide variety of extraordinary tourist sites: important archeological zones, beaches, majestic rivers, colonial-era architecture, canyons, jungles, forests, and flora and fauna that is extraordinary in its biodiversity. Restaurateurs, hoteliers, drivers, and millions of workers across other fields make their living from the tourism industry. According to INEGI, in 2016 there were 3,845,000 people employed in this crucial sector.

It is vitally important to combine development of the tourist industry with protection of the environment. That will entail sustainable garbage treatment, and the introduction of potable water, drainage systems, and specialized medical facilities in tourist zones. Simultaneously, we'll pursue public safety programs. In Mexico City, when we refurbished the Historic Center we installed cameras and a created a special police force.

D) Duty-free zones along the border

Our vision of development prioritizes creating meaningful employment for our citizens here in Mexico. Immigration, the informal economy, and illicit activities must cease to be the only options available for our people.

It is vital to ensure work opportunities and fair salaries throughout the nation. In recent decades, economic growth has produced drastic inequality; not only has the historic North-South divide persisted, but due to a lack of growth and employment, most of our country has steadily depopulated, primarily through migration to the United States on a historically unprecedented scale.

In the neoliberal period, as we've seen, growth rates have hovered around 2 percent per year. However, this is the national average, which doesn't account for the distribution of growth across the country. The relatively high growth rates in the tourist zones of the Caribbean and the Pacific, certain central and northern cities, and some border towns, which house *maquiladoras*, has masked the economic stagnation of the majority of the nation.

This is demonstrated by population growth in the interior and the extraordinary increase in migration to the United States. It is horrifying to see that from 1983 to the present, nearly half of our municipalities have decreased in population, and there has been a huge exodus toward a few key regions of our nation, accompanied by even larger migration flows out of the country. Examples abound of this wave of migration. Over a million inhabitants left the state of Veracruz in the last two decades in search of work in the border towns. Mexico today is simultaneously crowded and depopulated, characterized by marginalization and poverty, with small islets of growth that are nonetheless also being affected by the crisis.

It is imperative to support the economy of the border towns. As already noted, our development policies will bring people back to the countryside, but we cannot neglect the massive competitive advantage conferred by our proximity to the wealthiest nation in the world. The border cities and states of Tamaulipas, Nuevo León, Coahuila, Chihuahua, Sonora, and Baja California all face economic crisis, instability, and poor quality of life. Despite this, government neglect in these regions is notorious. Under Calderón, wildly expensive customs facilities were built that are now garish monuments to corruption; under Peña Nieto, VAT was raised along the border from 11 to 16 percent. One sees the decline in the *maquiladora* industry, which in twenty years, instead of growing has steadily lost out to Asian competitors. Researcher Marie-Laure Coubès, of Colegio de la Frontera Norte (College of the Northern Border), asserts that the economic crisis that began in the United States in 2009 had damaging effects on the labor market in Mexico. Focusing specifically on Tijuana, which used to provide employment opportunities for migrants from other regions of the country, the study notes that "the unemployment rate grew dramatically, from 2.1 percent to 4.0 percent and 7.2 percent between 2007, 2008, and 2009 respectively [...] From 2009 to present [2011], unemployment in Tijuana is greater than in other cities, which had been unprecedented in the past twenty years."[84]

To address this problem, we will create a duty-free zone along the northern border. We will consult with specialists and entrepreneurs to "avoid unnecessary regulation and the imposition of excessive levies to companies that wish to settle in the region," and consider "the establishment of a duty-free zone, much like those

---

84 Marie-Laure Coubès, "Recent hiring trends on the Northern border." Estudio-ponencia. México, El Colegio de la Frontera Norte.

in other regions such as China's coastal zone, a strategy that has allowed it to grow notably."[85]

Although we will present a specific platform in the near future, for now I will advance a few ideas for making the most of our trade agreements with the United States. We will employ a fiscal policy that reduces VAT and income taxes, and which promotes competitive prices with the United States in petroleum products and electricity. At the same time, we will move customs checks offices twenty kilometers inland; we will promote education, science, and technology; as well as fair incomes and social development (through urbanization, advancements in health, nurseries, and social security).

E) Increase salaries to drive up consumption in the internal market

It is essential to increase the purchasing power of the Mexican people through wage increases. Our minimum wage is inhumane and unconstitutional. The days of China's competitive advantage due to low labor costs are long gone; today Chinese workers earn more than our workers.

The neoliberal practice of limiting salary increases, on the pretext of fighting inflation, has led to impoverishment and the collapse of workers' purchasing power. According to Gerardo Esquivel, researcher at the College of Mexico, "the purchasing power of the minimum wage has diminished dramatically over the last few decades. By 2014, it had fallen 75 percent from its highest point (1976); it represents, in addition, a little over ⅓ of what it was 45 years ago (1969)."[86]

85 Isaac Sánchez-Juárez, Rosa María García, "Evaluation of the economic growth and employment along Mexico's Northern Border: The role of Public Investment" (Chihuahua: Universidad Autónoma de Ciudad Juárez, 2016), 173.

86 Gerardo Esquivel Hernández, "Extreme Inequality in Mexico: On the concentration of Economic and Political Power" (Mexico: Oxfam, June 2015), 29.

The most recent report from the Center for Multidisciplinary Analysis of UNAM[87] affirms that nineteen years ago, a minimum wage salary could purchase 51 kilograms of tortillas, or 250 pieces of white bread, or 12 kilograms of pinto beans; whereas today it can only pay for 6 kilograms of tortillas, or 38 pieces of white bread, or 4 kilograms of beans. According to their numbers, the decrease in purchasing power in this period has reached 78.71 percent.

Esquivel maintains that "one of the hardest aspects is that the true minimum wage in Mexico falls beneath the poverty line, and not only that, but twice below the line of extreme poverty. In real terms: a Mexican who works full time for minimum wage remains poor. If through this income he or she must support another family member, both are considered to be extremely poor. The salary is nowhere near enough to cover their basic nutritional needs. This is in conflict with the Constitution, which establishes that a minimum wage must guarantee a dignified quality of life. No other country in Latin America has seen its minimum wage lose so much purchasing power as has occurred in Mexico."[88]

This must be addressed immediately. Before presenting a concrete proposal, I want to reflect back on our history. In June 1906, while living in Toronto, Canada (where they sought refuge from *Porfirista* repression), Ricardo Flores Magón and Juan Sarabia wrote a work titled *The Program of the Liberal Party* and its accompanying manifesto. The document is brilliant, attuned to reality, proactive, and innovative. It is one of Mexico's most important documents, and should be widely read, though here we shall only summarize it briefly.

Their manifesto begins by proposing a radical change: replacing the dictatorship with authentic democracy. It argues for "the central aspirations of the people, and their most urgent needs": meaningful suffrage; an end to the practice of re-election; freedom

---

87   National Autonomous University of Mexico.

88   Isaac Sánchez-Juárez, Rosa María García, "Evaluation of the economic growth and employment along Mexico's Northern Border: The role of Public Investment."

of the press; due process; the prompt dispensation of justice; abolishment of the death penalty; an end to political cronyism and instead the strengthening of municipal autonomy; the closing of prisons and introduction of rehabilitative penitentiaries in their place; the elimination of obligatory military service; cooperation between Latin American states to defend themselves collectively; the affirmation of Reform laws and strict adherence to the Constitution; religious freedom; secular education; an increase in public schools; fair salaries for professors with special attention to the teaching of arts and trades. Furthermore, the manifesto calls for a reduction in taxes, with discounts for renters and those doing home and neighborhood improvements; and declares equal before the law legitimate and illegitimate children, as well as men and women.

The manifesto also lays out an extensive economic and social plan that balances liberty and prosperity; upholds respect for property rights and sets as its objective "to increase the general wealth"; it also sets forth policies for national development, particularly in agricultural and industrial sectors through the intervention of a democratic state that is prepared to distribute wealth, while shoring up internal demand. He argues clearly and convincingly: "The *pueblos* cannot prosper until the vast majority of people have some level of prosperity. A handful of millionaires hoarding wealth while millions starve produces not general well-being but well distributed misery, as we see in Mexico. In contrast, places where all can meet their basic needs will prosper, with millionaires or without them. The improvement of working conditions, on the one hand, and equitable distribution of land for cultivation, will confer innumerable advantages to the nation. Not only will this lift from poverty those who are most in need, but they'll support our nation's development of agriculture, industry, all sources of public wealth, all of which are stagnating due to widespread poverty. When the *pueblo* is too poor, when one's resources are scarcely enough to scrape by, he consumes only the essentials, and even these in minute quantities. When the millions of pariahs who today suffer hunger and cold are fed and warmed, demand will rise at a colossal scale and industry, agriculture, and commerce, will have the impetus to develop on a scale never before seen."[89]

It's clear that increasing the income of the majority benefits the populace as a whole. This shall be our guiding principle, and so we will pursue a gradual restoration of purchasing power, starting with an increase in the minimum wage and through gradual increases in base-level government salaries, of over at least three points above inflation per year. The percentage increase to the minimum wage must be evaluated and agreed upon, in due course, by labor and business representatives.

In October 2016, Enrique Cárdenas, of the Espinosa Yglesias Centre for Studies, wrote a superb article for *El Universal* titled "Minimum wage is not enough for the bare minimum." What follows is the complete article:

The establishment of Mexico's minimum wage took place upon the enactment of the Constitution of 1917. At that time, ours was one of the few countries that had implemented it: New Zealand did so in 1894, Australia in 1896, and the UK in 1910. Then, as I understand, came Mexico. The establishment of the minimum wage followed the massive loss of purchasing power of salaries throughout the armed conflict, and before long hyperinflation was unleashed. We've never experienced anything like it.

From then on, the minimum wage was defined as that which is sufficient for a worker to sustain his or her family with dignity, no more, no less. The minimum wage has been implemented in a variety of ways. From the '40s to the late '70s, salaries rose alongside worker productivity, leading to a growth in purchasing power. In 1969 it was 185 pesos per day (US$10) by today's prices. Today it's a mere 73 pesos. During the petroleum boom years, it increased to over 250 pesos per day (US$13.64) by today's prices, but in 1981 it dropped to 226 pesos (US$12.33). Following the debt crisis of 1982, and the massive inflation and macroeconomic contraction that followed, the

---

89 Ralph Roeder, *Hacia el México moderno: Porfirio Díaz II* (México: Fondo de Cultura Económica, 1973), 251–252.

minimum wage, at today's prices, collapsed to 71.50 pesos (US$3.90). During those years of high inflation, the government used salary control and its own influence to send market signals: it became an anchor to control inflation. Thus, purchasing power fell significantly. Finally, amid the macroeconomic stabilization after the 1994–95 crisis, minimum wage in real terms stagnated and sits at around 69 pesos per day (US$3.76), despite widespread gains in productivity. This has been the trajectory of the minimum wage for the past nearly fifty years.

But the important question is: Is this enough for one person and an economic dependent to live with dignity? To answer that, we must look at Coneval's data, which delineates the line of basic well-being (in terms of meeting basic nutritional needs) at 1,334 pesos per month (US$72.77) per person, and 2,702 pesos (US$147.39) in an urban environment, which includes other costs. Thus, the daily income a person must take in is 89 pesos (US$4.85), to cover food alone, or 180 pesos (US$9.82) if they are to cover other expenses in an urban environment. In other words: our minimum wage is 16 pesos (US$0.87) less than what is required to avoid starvation, and 107 pesos ($5.84) less than what is required to survive with a basic level of dignity.

Discussions around potential implementation have taken many tacks. Some contend that authorities and entrepreneurs have refused to provide a living wage; another argument is that it will create a spiral of inflation. If this was implemented on all salaries at all wage ranges, they would be right.

However, this "lighthouse effect"[90] too has an inverse. A boss who pays two times the minimum wage surely thinks he pays well; ultimately, it's double what the law demands. He doesn't consider that, even morally, he does them a disservice: two times the minimum wage, or 146 pesos (US$7.96) per day, is not enough for a person and their dependent to live with dignity. Thus, a minimum wage this low "pulls" other wages down with it. An increase in the minimum wage thus helps workers across the spectrum.

---

90   An economic phenomenon wherein minimum wage increases lead to increases across the economy, including in the informal sector.

In Mexico, from the 1970s up until 1982 the minimum wage was sufficient to live with dignity. From then onward, it's simply not enough. Why were employers able to afford these salaries in the past, yet argue today that it's not possible? Have we not advanced at all from those days? If our economy, the sixteenth largest in the world, can't handle these minimum wage increases, then something is very wrong. There is no rational reason for mandating that salaries remain beneath the poverty line.

*

I fully agree with Cárdenas, and I believe that it is economically, socially, and morally essential to increase our minimum wage, and I reiterate that I am certain we can negotiate a consensus between the working class and business owners. Negotiations aside, I pledge that by 2019 the wages of government employees will increase. By our calculations, for every one percentage point increase in the federal payroll, we will require 11.16 billion pesos (US$608 million); that is to say, our proposal will cost around 33 billion pesos (US$1.8 billion). Note that we're talking about proportional increases for workers who earn less than 200,000 pesos (US$10,900) per year, with most going to those who earn much less. These increases will target teachers, doctors, police officers, soldiers, and other public servants. In addition, it will be feasible to increase the salary of federal government workers by at least three percentage points, if some benefits, like year-end bonuses, meal vouchers, clothing allowances, and other benefits are provided in pesos instead.

I instituted a similar a policy when I was the mayor of Mexico City. We pledged to do this during our campaign and we delivered as promised. While high functionaries saw their inflated salaries reduced, baseline workers received increases of two points over inflation. This gave them a 10 percent increase in purchasing power in real terms, plus what they obtained through the provision of benefits that ceased to be administered by sometimes-dishonest functionaries. In short, this plan both improves working conditions and, at the same time, strengthens consumption and our internal market.

F) Invest in our youth

Dating back to the last election, I have insisted on the vital importance of standing by our youth. A hallmark of the neoliberal period has been the marginalization of our young people. Lacking opportunity, they have harbored resentment, frustration, and hate, which has fomented the chronic violence that plagues our country. We must provide our youth with opportunities to work and attend school, both because it is just but also to ensure the stability of Mexican society.

Our plan is similar to US president Franklin Delano Roosevelt's, who during the Great Depression created an economic bill of rights that included the right to useful and decently paid employment. Our program will be titled "Youth building the future": we will canvas homes to sign up young people to the program and incorporate them into schools and the workforce. We will re-establish the principle of free education at every age level. The state will guarantee that every student who is willing to study will have access to a decent education. No one will be turned away; we will aim to achieve full enrollment, and admissions exams that currently serve only to exclude most applicants will be abolished. We will end the status quo of insufficient public investment that results in calls for the privatization of higher education.

Before long, we'll be reaching millions of young men and women who would otherwise have faced a dark and uncertain future. The program has three principal objectives: integrating the youth into productive or academic activities to give them tools for a better life; combating unemployment and antisocial behavior; and accelerating the development of a reserve of young talent whose energy and productivity will be needed as we look forward to a period of major economic growth.

We propose to create programs that will target two youth groups:

- Approximately 300,000 young women and men who have been rejected from public universities but still wish to study. They will be integrated in the short term into a new education project. The numbers we plan to enroll in the program may change according to demand.
- Roughly 2,300,000 young people who have unsuccessfully sought employment, or who have given up the search for employment, will be integrated into the workforce.

Through this program we aim to support young people in middle and high school who are at risk of dropping out, so that they may continue their education.

This first group of 300,000 students will be supported through a scholarship of 29,000 pesos (US$1,581) per year per student. The budget will amount to 8.7 billion pesos (US$474 million) and will be equitably distributed to students across the nation.

The second group will be encouraged to find new job opportunities. These young people (alongside those who resume schooling) will seek out apprentice programs at small, medium, and large firms.

Once our young people are enrolled in this program, the government will attempt to place applicants at either private or public sector organizations. In the private sector, they'll find work in agriculture, fishery, tourism, industry, and in services. In the public sector, they'll find work in construction, forestry, the energy industry, in infrastructure maintenance, and in remodeling of parks and gardens, streets, and public buildings.

Through this work, our young people will learn under a manager, tutor, or government functionary, to whom the government will transfer the minimum wage for training. The firm and the young person must inform the government each month of their accomplishments in order for payments to continue.

We will implement measures to prevent corruption emerging within the program. Specifically, this employment program must not result in existing workers being replaced by subsidized workers. In order to prevent this, these youths will be paid at a rate of about 1.5 times the minimum wage. The cost for the scheme will run at about 99.4 billion pesos (US$5.4 billion) per year. Ensuring that our young people are actively engaged in work or in studies through such programs will be a valuable investment in Mexico's future.

Through this program our young people will learn important skills that will generate increases in productivity. In addition to improving the living conditions of millions of young people and their families, this government program will promote the training of a labor force of sufficient productivity that growth rates of 6 percent or more may become feasible.

In order to succeed, this program requires a three-way commitment:

- The state will provide the basic subsidy to students and young people who enter the workforce.
- Our youth will commit to study and work hard.
- The firms or organizations who receive these interns will commit to training them and accurately informing the government about their progress.

The program will be implemented toward the end of 2018, and the initial placement of youths will begin in 2019.

We will distribute economic resources efficiently, relying on secure payments to the institutions that train or educate these youths, reducing administrative costs wherever possible. Throughout the program, the government will continue to explore opportunities for integrating young people into economic activity, depending on the state of the economy and the job opportunities that arise, as well as the performance of those in the program.

This program will be beneficial in a variety of ways. It will reduce unemployment and increase school enrollment. With better training for the job force, current and potential future productivity will increase, creating a favorable environment for future economic activity. Keeping our youth engaged in productive activity will also distance them from antisocial behavior, thereby helping to mend our social fabric and cementing young people's sense of community, cooperation, respect, and responsibility.

The official unemployment rate in February 2016 was 3.93 percent. If our program were implemented, this rate could be reduced to nearly zero. This program will open doors for our young people that will enable us to work together toward a better future.

G) Universal coverage of telecommunications

The mismanagement of vested interests has prevented our nation from enjoying the benefits of developments in telecommunications. Our internet is overly expensive and needlessly slow. It is not unusual to see people from the countryside or in the city climbing up hills in order to try to get better coverage. The internet is only really available in state capitals and large cities, and even there access is unreliable. In Oaxaca, for example, the vast majority of its 570 municipalities lack internet. Fewer than half of these municipalities have phone service—indeed, phone service is inconsistent across the country. At most, 30 percent of the national territory is covered.

The state must take action to confront this problem, as it seriously impedes our economic development. Telecommunications are essential for strategic development. Therefore, we pledge to install broadband internet nationwide through the Federal Electricity Commission. Electrical grids will allow for the creation of fiber optic networks that will cover even the most remote parts of the country. Though we won't rule out the use of other technologies if they allow us to provide access in remote areas, what matters most is that this service supports education, culture, health, and well-being. Equally important is that nationwide access to internet will allow us to uphold the right of the Mexican people to be informed about national, local, and international affairs. We will provide free Wi-Fi along highways, in plazas, in schools, in hospitals, and in public spaces. We estimate that this program will cost 10 billion pesos (US$545 million), and after one year in office we expect to provide internet access for the entire nation.

Of course, this does not mean reneging on concessions owned by the telecommunications industry. Needless to say, we won't be expropriating Televisa, as was bizarrely rumored in 2006. Existing media outlets will be respected. New radio and television concessions will also be granted. We will ensure full freedom of expression, and government censorship will not be tolerated, as it was in the canceling of programs like those of José Gutiérrez Vivó and Carmen Aristegui. No one will be persecuted for their beliefs, and we will make the right to dissent a meaningful one. We will demonstrate the difference between authoritarianism and democracy.

4. State of well-being

The conservative claim that wealth accumulated in the hands of a few will conveniently trickle down to the many is false. It is woefully wrong to assert that the state must not promote development or address income inequality. It is equally wrong to suggest that by focusing our efforts on creating a climate favorable to investors we will de facto enjoy the fruits of those benefits as they spill over into the rest of society.

This type of thinking was accepted during the *Porfiriato*, and revolution was the inevitable result. In those times, people thought the state must only provide stability, that it must not intervene in economic affairs to promote the welfare of the people, because private initiative was believed to be more efficient. It was widely believed that the path to success could be found by granting licenses, concessions, and contracts, and by gaining the confidence of international investors by ensuring that they would receive high dividends.

Perhaps the greatest lesson from the *Porfirista* economic model is that economic progress without justice is impossible. The fatal flaw in such thinking is inability to grasp that the mere accumulation of wealth, without ensuring its equitable distribution, produces inequality and grave social turmoil. History has simply disproved the theory of so-called trickle-down economics.

The staggering failure of this policy can be seen across our impoverished regions nationwide. The decision to pursue the prosperity of the few came at the cost of the impoverishment of the vast majority of the Mexican people. It deepened inequality and produced our current state of social decay.

Poverty in Mexico is everywhere you look. It's in the northern states, which had previously been little affected. It's notorious in the densely populated areas and in our border states; in the countryside of Zacatecas, Nayarit, and Durango; it predominates in the center, in the south, and the southeast, and above all in indigenous communities. All over the country, our people lack job opportunities and find themselves forced to migrate and to abandon their families, customs, and traditions. Production for self-consumption, government support programs, and remittances from families abroad provide barely enough to survive. There's never enough to eat well, or for transportation, medical attention, gas, electricity—much less for entertainment or cultural recreation.

The social programs implemented under Salinas, Zedillo, Fox, Calderón, and Peña Nieto have been mere palliatives for poverty, if not perverse mechanisms for electoral control and manipulation.

According to the World Bank, some 60 million Mexicans are in poverty, of which 22.3 million are extremely poor—people who cannot afford to meet even their basic nutritional needs. Mexico has become one of the poorest countries on the continent, and has among the highest levels of inequality worldwide. Among the legions of forgotten and oppressed Mexicans, the very poorest are the nearly 10 million indigenous people.

In his widely-cited *Extreme Inequality in Mexico*, Gerardo Esquivel Hernández asserts that, while 38 percent of the indigenous population "lives in extreme poverty, the percentage corresponding to the total population is under 10 percent. This implies that extreme poverty rates for indigenous people are four times higher than that of the general population. When those living in moderate poverty are added to the formula, we learn that three out of every four speakers of an indigenous language are living in poverty. This data contrasts notably with the wider population, where at least half of the population is considered poor."[91]

In truth, not only has the state stopped promoting economic growth and job creation, but it has failed to meet its social responsibility to ensure the well-being of the Mexican people. Throughout the neoliberal period, investment in hospitals, schools, and universities all but ceased. On February 3, 1983, our Constitution was amended to grant the right to health care, and yet more than three decades later half of the population lacks access to social security. Here is an interesting paradox: since the right to health care was included in our Constitution, the public resources devoted to health care have declined in real terms. Put differently, what the law accomplished in theory, the budget eliminated in practice. One of the worst signs of governmental neglect and inequality is the lack of access to health services. In rural parts of states like Chiapas, Guerrero, or Oaxaca, mortality among young children is four times higher than in Nuevo León or Mexico City.

At the national level, nearly 4 million people inhabit houses with dirt floors, 9.7 million live in households with no drainage or sanitation system, and nearly 10 million lack potable water. In the countryside, nearly half of all households are overcrowded. Worse still, there is widespread hunger and malnutrition: 28 million Mexicans experience moderate to severe food insecurity.

As for education, Mexico lags behind many other countries. The number of those fifteen years or older who lack basic education is 40 percent, and the illiteracy rate is 5.5 percent. In more marginalized states like Oaxaca, Guerrero, or Chiapas, the rate of illiteracy is as high as 14.8 percent. The government's "education reforms" do not address the lack of opportunities to study or the poor quality of the education that currently exists. It seeks instead to render teachers helpless and to transfer the costs of education to parents, thereby normalizing the government's failure to guarantee the right to free public education for all.

91 Gerardo Esquivel Hernández. op. cit., p. 32.

Our corrupt politicians are completely unconcerned with the right to public education. They do nothing to combat the roots of the problem: hunger and poverty. Neither are they interested in improving our educational infrastructure. According to recent data, 48 percent of public schools don't have adequate drainage; 31 percent lack potable water; 12.8 percent lack bathrooms; and 11.2 percent are without electricity.[92]

So-called "education reform" serves to eliminate public school teachers through incessant evaluations and the privatization of education. It is wholly untrue that teachers are opposed to being examined in good faith, as they have repeated time and time again; what they reject is the cynical use of these tests to justify arbitrary cuts to education funding.

The main issues to be tackled are the poor quality of education in our schools and the high student dropout rate. Both problems are rooted in poverty and hunger. In middle to advanced education there is a profound lack of staff, infrastructure, and basic equipment such as desks and lockers. Here, the exclusionary character of the neoliberal model is highly visible.

More dramatic still is the situation in higher education. In Mexico, only 29.1 percent of people between the ages of eighteen and twenty-four have access to advanced education. UNESCO has suggested a target of 40 to 50 percent. This means that we must dramatically increase the number of higher education slots available to young people in the next few years if we want to meet such a target.

We need an urgent change in policy to guarantee the right to free education for all Mexicans. We must not permit exclusion through admissions exams; the state must guarantee the right to public, free, high quality education at every age group.

For the past thirty years, and as a result of our government's abandonment of higher education, enrollment in private schools increased from 16 to 37 percent. We do not oppose private education, but we stand emphatically against the abandonment of public

92 Gerardo Esquivel Hernández.

education. The market can take care of those with the money to pay for private schooling, but the state has a duty to guarantee the right to free education for all.

If our commitment to education continues to decline at the current level—or if education is placed in the hands of the market—the number of dropouts will continue to grow. The main problem isn't the quality of education, but the problem of access. Although tuition fees may appear to be low, at between 3,000 and 5,000 pesos per month (US$163–272), one must recall that 38.9 percent of the working population earns income of less than 4,206 pesos (US$229) per month. There is a dark agenda behind the state's neglect of education. Their hope is that education will cease to be a vehicle for social mobility, and that it will become, instead, an instrument to sustain an ideological framework that privileges the pursuit of profit and that fosters rampant inequality. Education has increasingly become the preserve of the privileged few, and withholding it from the masses has come at the price of social decay.

For the good of all, first serve the poor

Our first priority must be serving the poor. Only through the creation of a just society will we achieve the revitalization of Mexico. Our country will not be respected internationally if poverty and inequality persist. It is both an ethical imperative and a necessity for ensuring the stability of Mexican society. There can be no peace without justice. Fostering feelings of kinship or fellowship is the most efficient way of guaranteeing the rule of law and a governable populace. Nothing justifies the abject poverty that millions of Mexicans endure; this is neither the product of fate or destiny. The neoliberal experiment has churned out damaged subjects; poverty has remained entrenched and even worsened in the absence of a state with a real social vision.

We must recognize, although it flies in the face of neoliberal dogma, that in any nation the state is fundamental to the population's well-being, and that in a nation like ours, with so much inequality, it is essential to the survival of many. We can't keep social justice off the government's agenda. It is the worst injustice to use the state to defend special interests, but then refuse to use the state's capacity to secure the well-being of the majority. It is indefensible to use the authority of the state to rescue financial institutions that face bankruptcy but refuse to use the state for promoting the well-being of the most impoverished.

The state must work decisively toward social development. It must promote economic growth and the creation of jobs to improve the economic situation of our people. This will result in better education, health, and overall quality of life. At the same time, as this level of development is pursued, and given the extreme poverty in which the majority of Mexicans live, the state must guarantee a basic measure of well-being for all.

Our program in this area consists of establishing a Welfare State, to guarantee that the poor, the weak, and the forgotten find protection amid economic uncertainty and attendant social inequality and disadvantage, so that we can all live without fear or anxiety. The Welfare State will protect people at all stages of life, from cradle to grave, ensuring the public's right to food, work, health, education, culture, housing, and social security. This will require an investment of 50 billion additional pesos (US$2.7 billion) per year.

I propose the following:

- We must eradicate hunger and enshrine the right to food in our Constitution.
- We must recognize work as fundamentally fulfilling, when premised upon respect for the rights of workers, and the creation of suitable jobs for those who enter the workforce.
- We must protect nature and our natural resources to ensure the sustainability of life on Earth.
- We must guarantee rights for women, children, and young people, the disabled, the elderly, and those of all sexual orientations and genders.
- We must care for vulnerable and at-risk populations, and support those with disabilities, single mothers, and migrants.

- We must guarantee the right to education and health as universal rights, free and of good quality.
- We must establish a universal pension for elderly adults and a redistributive retirement system, doubling the pension that is received at present and granting this support as well to retirees and pensioners from the IMSS[93] and ISSSTE.[94]
- We must recognize the autonomy of indigenous communities in order to help them preserve their identity and culture, enrich their collective lives, and preserve the resources under their care, incorporating the San Andrés Accords[95] without omissions or changes whatsoever.
- We must promote the right to adequate housing. Millions of Mexicans live in substandard housing and lack access to basic services. Therefore we will pursue the construction of low income housing to guarantee this right and to generate millions of jobs in construction.
- We must assert the right to the city, and its concomitant obligations like stability, infrastructure, access to services, health, education, and work.

We will also elevate science, culture, and sports, which have been relegated to the sidelines in the agendas of previous governments. In 2012, we proposed the creation of the Secretariat of Culture, which is now in operation. We must create similar departments for science, technology, research and innovation, and sport. As in nearly everything else, our lack of investment in sports is glaringly evident. At the last Olympic Games in Río de Janeiro, Brazil, our country performed poorly; placing sixty-first in the medal table despite being the tenth largest economy in the world. Yet we win gold medals for corruption, inequality, migration, and violence.

93 Mexican Social Security Institute.

94 Institute for Social Security and Services for State Workers.

95 An agreement between the Zapatista Army and the Mexican government, granting autonomy to the indigenous people of Mexico.

Education isn't a privilege, it's a right

Education means equality. It strengthens the spirit, improves one's quality of life, spurs development, and makes democracy possible. Education benefits all of us. The right to education must be made available to people of all ages and all social classes. Students must be provided with a safe, decent environment in which to study. I believe that it is the responsibility of the state to expand the right to education across all age groups, from preschool to university. This requires the commitment to invest in infrastructure and educational resources, but also to support students by helping to provide transportation, uniforms, meals, scholarships, and, where necessary, housing, so that no economic or familial situation will impede their access to any level of education.

We must eradicate illiteracy and ensure that those who want to pursue basic education are able to do so. We must invest in public libraries across the nation. The basis of democratic stability is an informed and engaged populace who are well equipped to participate in the democratic process. The right to literacy is essential to guarantee that the 40 million Mexicans who today lack access to education, or have had to abandon their education for economic reasons, are able to participate as equal citizens.

We must put an end to the segregation and exclusion that characterizes indigenous and rural education. It's urgent that indigenous peoples, so central to our identity, have the needed resources to preserve their languages, their collective cohesion, their culture, and their autonomy. Rural and indigenous education must use ancestral knowledge to help us reclaim our values, our cultural memories, and our knowledge as a *pueblo* and as a nation.

We must eradicate the privileged and private use of public resources. Teachers across the country must have the right to dignified working conditions, with a reasonable salary and benefits. Working in tandem with parents, they will ensure that free, high quality education is guaranteed to all children, and they will work to prevent any kind of abuse of our students. Teachers will have the freedom of association and expression, as well as the right to freely elect their union leaders. To repair the current poor state of our education system, it is essential to initiate a process of continuous training, active participation in reform programs, and substantive improvements in working conditions in teacher-training schools[96] and universities.

We must ensure access for those with disabilities, and overcome the regime of segregation to which they are currently subjected, which prioritizes neither their integration nor the development of their potential.

We must increase our efforts in the realms of art and physical education. We shall create, nurture, and multiply the physical, intellectual, emotional, and creative capacities of students.

We must substantially increase our budget for scientific research, especially that which is targeted toward advanced education. And we must promote the production and exchange of knowledge that will support preservation efforts on behalf of our environmental and cultural heritage. We will promote the development of basic and applied sciences, utilizing, while also protecting, our natural resources. We must also stand firm in the defense of our identity and sovereignty.

5. Safe society

In a democratic state, the promotion of public safety is essential to the guaranteeing of life, property, and peace of mind for all, not just for a privileged few. The crisis of public safety and violence that we face today is the product of a poorly conceived war on drugs that relies solely on coercive means. The security crisis that plagues Mexico is a result of a confluence of factors: poverty, injustice, and exclusion, aggravated by the inefficiency of the authorities and corruption within the police and the judiciary.

The country cannot continue to put up with government-enabled criminal impunity. The government must investigate all violations of human rights. Those violations include tragedies such

---

96 Known as "normal schools," often hotbeds of progressive political activity.

as the assassination and disappearance of young *normalistas*[97] of Ayotzinapa, and the killings of Apatzingán, Tanhuato, Ostula, and Tlatlaya. Other atrocities, such as the forced disappearance of people by state representatives or individuals under their protection, must also be investigated.

I emphasize that violence is, in large part, a product of the neglect of our youth. They have been denied a future, and are effectively barred from employment or schooling. It should surprise no one that they turn toward antisocial behavior.

By necessity, millions of young people have migrated in recent times. Because of a lack of opportunity, they have opted to cross the border, risking their lives to do so. However, others who have stayed behind have been lured into organized crime. Testimonies abound of young people who are conscious of the risks they run by making that decision, yet they prefer a life of crime to marginalization and poverty. It's horrific to know that young people populate the ranks of organized crime, and that the majority of the 159,472 assassinations during Calderón's term and during Peña Nieto's term so far (up to August 2015, not including the 26,000 people who have disappeared, according to official data) have been of young people from poor families.

However, neoliberal governments and the elites in power refuse to accept that poverty and a lack of job opportunities has created this crisis of hate and resentment. They have completely neglected to address the root causes of crime. On the contrary, they have sought to resolve the problem solely through coercive means, meeting violence with violence, as if one could successfully counter evil with more evil.

We must combat this hypocritical and conservative mindset by confidently asserting that instability and violence can only be defeated by making profound changes in our social fabric. To

97 A student who attends a teacher training school. In September 26, 2014, forty-three students went missing. It is alleged that they were handed over to the *Guerreros Unidos* cartel with the full cooperation of Iguala mayor José Luis Abarca Velázquez.

create a more humane society, we must combat inequality, thereby erasing the frustration and societal tensions it engenders.

In addition to addressing these root causes, it is necessary to eradicate corruption across all branches of the military, the police, public ministries, and the judiciary. I propose four specific actions that we must undertake to combat this scourge of violence and bring peace to our nation:

- We must combat and eradicate corruption in every facet of government. Corruption allows organized crime to thrive and prosper. Many major crimes could not be accomplished without the collusion of public functionaries. Narcotrafficking, the escape of drug lords from jails, the theft of gasoline, money laundering, arms trafficking, and other illicit practices invariably take place with the complicity of corrupt authorities. We must have zero tolerance for criminal collusion.
- We must establish specialized security bodies in charge of combating minor crime. Combating organized crime requires intelligence more than strength. Intelligent police work should be prioritized over coercion.
- We must coordinate a meaningful response to the scourge of violence. We can't take on organized crime without first being organized ourselves. When I served as the mayor of Mexico City, we worked together with the public ministry, the chief of police, and government representatives.
  Every day at 6 a.m., including on the weekend, our team—the mayor, the attorney general, the secretary of government, the secretary of public security, the legal advisor, and other cabinet functionaries—convened to report on the past twenty-four hours and to respond to the latest developments. Public servants across the region did the same.
- In accordance with the laws of national security, the state councils will meet daily to share information and decide on policy. The governor, the representative of the Interior

Ministry, the Attorney General's Office, the commander of the military and naval departments, the secretary of government, of security, the state attorney general, and the president of the Court of Law shall be invited, as will members of civil society.

- The Army and the Marines will join in our efforts to guarantee public safety. The fundamental objective of the armed forces is to safeguard our territory and preserve Mexico's sovereignty. However, under present circumstances it is essential that we add the preservation of our internal stability to their charter. We must take advantage of the trained and experienced personnel that we have in order to guarantee the right of all Mexicans to live without fear or anxiety. The democratic government of Mexico will defend the country's sovereignty, but our priority will be maintaining peace. In the unlikely case of armed aggression from an outside force, not only will the army be mobilized, but so will many of the people rise up to defend the country, as has happened throughout Mexico's history. We will end state repression, and no one will be subjected to torture, assassination, or forced disappearance by political or military institutions. The Army and the Navy will serve to protect the Mexican people. We will study the feasibility of creating a National Guard comprising 220,000 soldiers and 30,000 marines who will remain organized under the command of the armed forces. We will take advantage of the knowledge, the discipline, and the material resources of our armed forces to secure the safety of the Mexican people.

I would argue that unless and until we address the issue of public safety, all other government action will fall short. But I also want to stress that we will not employ coercive measures to take on the grave problem of instability and violence. The belief that the deterioration of our social fabric can be combated only through the use of force is profoundly wrong and highly dangerous, as Mexican history amply demonstrates. The law must be followed, without question, but without social reforms and the strengthening of our values, we cannot put a stop to crime, violence, and societal decomposition.

I'm convinced that the fight against delinquency is more than a matter of cops and robbers. The radical solution, the one that gets to the root of the problem (and that is also the most efficient and least expensive), is to combat unemployment, poverty, family disintegration, the decline of values, and the absence of opportunity. Therefore, to ensure public safety, social development is essential. I would conclude by pointing out that the crisis of instability and violence has been exacerbated, too, by the example of our elites (and their extravagant lifestyles), for whom money rules above all else. There is no way out of our problems without a comprehensive renewal of Mexico's civic life. That renewal entails, above all, the creation of a new way of thinking, reinforced with our values of dignity, honesty, and compassion for our fellow citizens.

6. A Benevolent Republic

As I've already expounded on the themes of honesty and justice, I will now address the concept of a fraternal republic, an idea that I have been developing over the course of recent years. In my opinion, the societal decadence with which we now contend is the result of the lack of opportunities for advancement, and the loss of cultural, moral, and spiritual values. Therefore, my proposal for achieving the revitalization of Mexico begins by promoting justice and, at the same time, creating a new mode of living based on love for family, our fellow citizens, nature, our country, and humanity.

Human beings have certain basic needs. No one can be happy without work, food, health, or housing. People mired in poverty are forced to focus on survival, not on political, scientific, artistic, or spiritual pursuits. But life must not be reduced merely to the accumulation of material things. Often the unscrupulous pursuit of success at any cost leads to an empty and dehumanized life. Therefore we seek an equilibrium between material and spiritual needs: we seek a society in which no one will lack the essentials to survive and in which love for our fellow human beings may flourish.

Central to creating this fraternal republic will be regenerating Mexico's public life through a new way of practicing politics by elevating three essential values: honesty, justice, and love. By practicing honesty and justice we will improve our living conditions and achieve peace; and by imbuing our actions with love we will promote that which is good in ourselves, which will aid us in the pursuit of happiness. As I've pointed out more than once, the current crisis is not rooted only in a lack of material goods, but also in a loss of values. For that reason, it's essential to practice a new way of thinking that will instill love for one's family, one's neighbors, for nature, and for our country.

Social decomposition must not only be combated through development and the promotion of well-being. Taking action to improve our material well-being is important, but it is not everything: it is urgent, too, to develop our humanitarian impulses. José Martí, in his prologue to the book *The Importance of Doing Nothing* by Oscar Wilde, says he finds "abominable those towns which, through cultivation of material goods, forget the spiritual ones, that lighten life's heavy loads and predispose one to hard work and effort."[98]

Building on the moral and cultural reserves that still exist in the families and communities of Mexico, buoyed by the inherent goodness of our people, we must undertake the task of pushing back against the cult of individualism, which neglects the values that equate well-being with the collective good.

I recognize that it may be controversial, but I believe that we cannot address the problem at its roots without putting moral revitalization at the center of our efforts. We must achieve a revolution in public ethics if we are to transform Mexico. Only then will we be able confront the individualism, greed, and hate that has led to

---

98 Oscar Wilde, *The Critic as Artist (Upon the Importance of Doing Nothing and Discussing Everything)* (Mondial, 2007).

our decline as a nation. Those who believe that this is not the realm of politics forget that the ultimate aim of politics is to foster love and well-being, because this is the basis of happiness. In 1776, the US Declaration of Independence established the pursuit of happiness as a fundamental right and asserted that defending this right was one of the government's responsibilities. The first article of the French Constitution of 1793 establishes communal happiness as the aim of society. Article 24 of our Apatzingán Constitution (1814) notes: "The happiness of the *pueblo* and its people is rooted in equality, safety, property, and liberty. The aim of governments is the protection of these rights."

From the Old Testament up to today, justice and fellowship have occupied a central place in the study of ethics. The first books of the Bible make several references to the importance of caring for the weak and oppressed. For example, regarding the tribute that should be offered to Yahweh, we read: "The second he shall then prepare as a burnt offering according to the law. [...] But if his means are insufficient for this offering, then he shall bring two turtledoves or two young pigeons. And if his means are insufficient for two turtledoves or two young pigeons, then for his offering for that which he has sinned, he shall bring the tenth of an ephah of fine flour" (Leviticus). In addition, there are appeals to protect the vulnerable: "If you lend money to my people, to the poor among you, you are not to act as a creditor to him; you shall not charge him interest" (Exodus). Among other prescriptions for moral character, we read: "If there is a poor man with you, [...] you shall not harden your heart, nor close your hand from your poor brother; but you shall freely open your hand to him, and shall generously lend him sufficient for his need in whatever he lacks" (Deuteronomy).

The New Testament affirms that Jesus of Nazareth expressed his love for the poor and vulnerable. In the Sermon on the Mount, he said: "Blessed are the poor, for theirs is the kingdom of heaven." His words were threatening to the powerful, and they accused him of inciting revolt. These ethical and social precepts can be found in the teachings of prophets and wise men of all religions. Indeed, in the words of Confucius: "To put the world in order, we must first put the nation in order; to put the nation in order, we must first put the family in order; to put the family in order; we must first cultivate our personal life; we must first set our hearts right." Buddha, for his part, said: "If with a pure mind a person speaks or acts, happiness follows them like a never-departing shadow."

But these precepts of justice and kindness have also been espoused by secular thinkers since the time of antiquity. Aristotle professed: "Political science spends most of its efforts on making the citizens to be of a certain character, that is, good and capable of noble acts."

In more recent times, on our continent, we speak of revolutionaries, partisans not only of justice but of goodness. Eduardo Galeano, in one of his final books, *Children of the Days*, describes an exemplary man by the name of Rafael Barrett, who "spent more time in jail than at home, and died in exile," and tended to repeat the phrase "If the good does not exist, we shall have to invent it." And closer to home, our own Ricardo Flores Magón wrote from a prison in Los Angeles to his beloved Maria, his "gentle creature." This anticlerical, upright man, who thought only of justice and revolution, made clear that "being firm is very different from being unreasonable," and wrote beautiful love notes asking his beloved to walk by the jail, in hopes of seeing her "dear sweet face" from his cell. He also wrote: "The group from Chicago won't defend us. We are just poor Mexicans. That is our crime. Our skin is not white and they cannot understand that underneath dark skin too there are nerves, there is a heart and a brain." He does not see any separation between love and his cause, and confesses: "I'm unsatisfied with my lack of communication, because I can't speak to you. I'm not satisfied, nor will I be. I can't sigh at your ear, my love, or take in your breath or see your enchanting face up close . . . Anyone who sees me will say I don't suffer; instead, I suffer quietly. I don't want anyone to feel for me." At the end of the day, as Silvio Rodríguez says, "A good revolutionary is only moved by love."

This profound sensitivity is an inherent part of our *pueblo*. Four years ago, when a family member was hospitalized in the National Institute of Respiratory Illnesses, I met a young boy named

Chuchín. He was born prematurely and required around-the-clock medical attention. He couldn't eat solids after a tracheotomy, and was instead fed through a tube. He never knew the outside word. He spent three years living in that hospital. His parents were poor laborers from Xochimilco. This boy was treated by the staff with all the love he deserved. He was adored by the cleaning staff, social workers, nurses, doctors, guards, and directors. On Children's Day, Three Kings Day, and on his birthday, they'd celebrate with cake, toys, and presents. He enjoyed the love of all who surrounded him throughout his too-short life.

This is what I mean when I speak of elevating and propagating these feelings. We already have them: we need merely to cultivate them. However, there are some who assert that discussing our spiritual values equates to meddling in religious affairs. Alfonso Reyes addresses this objection masterfully in his *Moral Primer*: the good is not only desirable for believers, but in general for all people; the good is not only based off the reward one will receive in heaven, but for reasons relevant here on earth.

A collective that does not protect its weakest members condemns itself to oblivion, because it weakens the links that bind it together and creates a dog-eat-dog culture, thereby leaving individual members vulnerable and the community in danger of disintegration.

In the towns of Oaxaca, for example, many community members follow their religious beliefs and serve on public works or government positions without receiving a salary, motivated only by the principle that one should help others.

We therefore aim to contribute to the formation of happy and good men and women, based on the premise that being good is the only way to be happy. Happiness is not found through hoarding wealth, titles, or fame, but through harmony with our conscience, ourselves, and our neighbors.

Deep and lasting happiness cannot be gained through fleeting pleasures. These provide joy only in the moment, but once they end one is left feeling empty. When one attempts to satisfy oneself with those fleeting pleasures, vice and corruption are frequently the result, which makes us unhappier still. Therefore, we must focus on the good, on love and on harmony for these are the joys that keep tension and frustration at bay. José Martí said that by taming ourselves, one forges character, creates joy and renders life beautiful. Therefore, it's important that each of us has a personal moral code, reflecting our beliefs, our history, and social circumstances.

Reyes, in his *Moral Primer*, explores general precepts of morality from the most specific to the most generalized. We can imagine them, he writes, like a series of concentric circles; we start from the inside and work our way out. According to Reyes, there are six precepts that comprise basic goodness: respect for ourselves in body and spirit; respect for family; respect for country; respect for the human race; and respect for the environment.

Long before Reyes, Leo Tolstoy, in his book *My Religion*, listed five conditions for happiness on earth: the sky, the sun, fresh air, and nature; the work we do that we've chosen freely; familial harmony; free communion with people; good health and a painless death.

Of course there are other precepts that must be followed: honesty, justice, thrift, liberty, dignity, equality, fraternity, and the rule of law. To this we must add more modern rights and principles, such as diversity, nondiscrimination, and the right to free speech and personal sovereignty.

In short, these prerequisites for a fraternal republic must become our moral code. To facilitate this, we are committed to creating a moral Constitution, with the help of specialists in their fields: philosophers, psychologists, sociologists, anthropologists, and others who have something meaningful to contribute: indigenous elders, teachers, parents, young people, writers, poets, businessmen, activists, people of all religious backgrounds, freethinkers, and atheists.

Once this moral Constitution has been developed and articulated, we will promote these values whenever possible. This moral Constitution will appear in schools, in the home, on radio, TV, and on social media. Older people who receive the right to a just pension will be invited to participate, if they so choose, to give advice on cultural, civic, and spiritual values.

Ultimately, our goal is to put a halt to the political and moral corruption that is destroying us as a society and as a nation. En route to this, we will establish the foundation for a world based on love and harmony, in full pursuit of true happiness.

¡Oye, Trump! Speech 10

Those Who Flee Violence

Laredo, Texas, March 28, 2017

Laredo's history is fascinating. It's the most Mexican city in the United States. Founded in the colonial era, Laredo is as old as El Paso and San Antonio. Before the arrival of Anglo-Saxon colonizers, these lands were populated by ranchers and migrants of Mexican ancestry. Just as in Tamaulipas, Nuevo León and Coahuila, families with Spanish surnames predominated: Garza, González, Salinas, Benavides, Cadena, Treviño, Elizondo, Longoria, Rodríguez, Martínez, Hinojosa, among others. Following the US invasion and expropriation of over half of our national territory, one of the most moving episodes of Mexican history took place here in Laredo. Due to the treaties imposed in 1848, the border ceased to be Río Nueces, in the north, and was moved south, to the Río Bravo. This resulted in Laredo, situated on the northern bank of the river, becoming part of the United States. However, the population of Laredo revolted because they wanted to remain a part of Mexico. The people convened a plebiscite, and those who refused to change their nationality won by a large majority. They must have said, as that Tigres del Norte song goes, "I didn't cross the border, the border crossed me." But the US did not acknowledge the results of the referendum and in defense of their freedom and nationality, seventeen families from Laredo moved to the other side of Río Bravo and established Nuevo Laredo, Mexico. It is said that they brought even their dead with them. What is certain is that the bonds of friendship remained intact between residents on both sides of the Río Bravo. For a great stretch of time the border was purely notional.

Even with the passage of time, Laredo remained home to the Mexican people. This city became the refuge of Mexican revolutionaries. In the *Porfiriato*, according to historian José Valades, Laredo was a "hotbed for the enemies of the *Porfirista* regime." Doctor Ignacio Martínez, who published the newspaper *El Mundo*, took refuge here until Porfirio Díaz's and Bernardo Reyes's[99] gunmen assassinated him in front of the Texas-Mexican train station. Paulino Martínez, another upstanding journalist, fled to this city as well. Catarino Garza Rodríguez, the Mexican revolutionary, organized his guerillas here eighteen years before Francisco Madero[100] took up arms. The Flores Magón brothers, Camilo Arriaga, Santiago de la Hoz and Juan Sarabia crossed the border to publish their newspaper, *Regeneración*.[101] Madero passed through upon his escape from the San Luis Potosí jail to meet his followers in San Antonio and agitate for revolution from this side of the border. Laredo has been a cornerstone of our history, and it has always espoused tolerance and protection for social justice advocates, journalists, and opposition candidates. We are therefore certain that Donald Trump's anti-immigrant stance will not take hold here. Given the city's historic solidarity with Mexico, we chose to end our migrant support tour here. Over two months, in support of the *pueblos* of Mexico, we visited Los Angeles, Chicago, El Paso, Phoenix, New York, Washington, San Francisco, and now, Laredo. Here, we choose to address the sad cases of those who have sought to escape the violence that plagues our country and have taken refuge in the United States.

The rise of neoliberalism over the last thirty years (which has entailed privatization, abandonment of our rural areas, economic stagnation, unemployment, neglect of our youth, inequality, and corruption) ushered in the crisis of violence and instability that plagues us today.

This corruption and looting of the Mexican economy by the rich has left the Mexican people with only three choices: attempt to

---

99 A Mexican general who served under Díaz. Díaz later appointed him governor of Nuevo León.

100 Mexican revolutionary who sparked the Mexican revolution and succeeded Porfirio Díaz after his reign of seven terms.

101 Mexican anarchist newspaper founded by the Flores Magón brothers; official mouthpiece of the Mexican Liberal Party.

survive in the informal economy; migrate to the United States; or survive through criminal activity.

The majority have opted to pursue an honest living, but hundreds of thousands, especially young people, have had no choice but to resort to crime. These are the roots of the crisis of instability and violence that now plagues our country.

When the government abandoned its duties to our people, criminal elements took control of huge areas of our country. They accumulated vast economic power and brought with them terror, extortion, and death.

Their violence provoked a new wave of refugees. No longer were migrants fleeing just hunger and poverty; now they fled death. In the North, entire *pueblos* were abandoned amid the chaos. Many have had to flee to avoid forced recruitment by the cartels. Others were forced to escape after losing family members to the violence.

Across the country, the mere act of reporting a crime or angering the wrong person is cause enough to flee one's home. The number of refugees fleeing insecurity has increased like never before during the neoliberal age.

The official statistics regarding the number of people displaced aren't reliable because the authorities are reluctant to disclose their data, and those who are forced to flee rarely report on their situation for fear of reprisal. The National Human Rights Commission stated, in May 2016, that it had registered 35,344 cases of displacement due to violence, of which 60 percent were in Tamaulipas. The National Survey of Demographic Dynamics (ENADID) affirmed that between 2009 and 2014, at least 236,800 people fled their homes due to threats of instability. Laura Rubio, investigator for the Mexico Autonomous Institute of Technology (ITAM) has stated that the numbers are closer to 281,000.

According to a report by the Pro Migrant Defense Coalition, between 2013 and 2016 the "Madre Asunta" shelter in Tijuana took in 1,106 women seeking asylum in the US due to violence.

A study by Syracuse University in New York found that between 2005 and 2010, US authorities received 2,400 asylum requests from Mexicans. From 2011 to 2016, this number ballooned to 12,000.

But only a small number of those who flee violence and insecurity to the US formally request asylum, therefore the total number may be much larger.

Ultimately, it's clear that Calderón's declaration of a "war on crime" and his criminally absurd decision to use indiscriminate military force only aggravated the violence and instability. It's clear, too, that the current government has been incapable of untangling itself from this counterproductive and foolish policy. The results of this failed strategy are all around us: in the ten years since the beginning of Calderón's rule, 210,000 people have been murdered and over one million people have been victims of violence.

It is outrageous that neoliberal politicians and elites will not recognize that poverty and a lack of job opportunities are the root causes of this crisis. And, as is obvious, they have no plans to address the root causes. On the contrary, they plan to resolve our problems through coercive measures, meeting violence with more violence, as if fire could be extinguished with flames.

We maintain that the solution to violence and instability must take two forms: combating corruption from the highest levels on down, and the effective delivery of the rights to work, to education, to health, to housing, to sport, and to culture. If it keeps employing brute force, the government will cause violence to multiply rather than eradicating it. Instead of earmarking greater and greater amounts of money toward arms purchases, we must put these resources toward job creation, the construction of advanced education facilities, and the promotion of well-being. Only in this way can we address the root causes of Mexico's security crisis; only then can we restore the rule of law throughout our country.

Just as it is right and necessary to guarantee the right to work and to well-being, so, too, we must offer the opportunity to return to those who have been forced to flee violence and crime. We must ensure that no one will be forced to flee their homes because their lives are in danger.

It is a great source of pride that we are accompanied by Elena Poniatowska, the greatest author in Mexico, not only because of her literary talent but because of her enormous goodness and deep love for our people.

Despite the struggles we face today, Mexico has a movement of passionate men and women who, sooner rather than later, will realize the ideals of justice, dignity, liberty, fraternity, democracy, and sovereignty for which we all yearn.

CHAPTER 10
A GLIMPSE AT 2024

If we are victorious in 2018 and enact the changes I've proposed, by the end of my term Mexican society will have achieved a wholly new level of well-being. Reduced unemployment and increased prosperity will result from our new economic policies, in tandem with economic development, greater public safety, and the strengthening of our cultural, moral, and spiritual values.

Once we have achieved an average growth rate of 4 percent during our term in office, we will have outdone the record of the neoliberal experiment. Recall that from 1983 to 2016, while our population increased by 2 percent annually, the economy grew by just 2.03 percent. Things will be different under our administration: the population will increase by 1.7 percent and the economy by 4 percent. We will finally and decisively overcome neoliberal stagnation.

In 2024 we will grow by 6 percent; by then our jobs program will be fully realized. There will be less unemployment, a more skilled job force, more demand for workers, and, ultimately, higher salaries.

Our fields will be productive like never before; by the middle of our term of office we will achieve self-sufficiency in corn and beans; by 2024, we will be self-sufficient in rice. Beef, pork, poultry, and eggs will follow, and milk imports will decline considerably. We'll export more fruit, vegetables, and legumes. Production of papaya, coffee, bananas, and cacao will have increased. In short, we will reverse the commercial deficit of the agricultural sector.

We will have reforested our national territory and guaranteed the conservation of the natural environment. We will have restored rivers, *arroyos*, and lakes, and treated wastewater, and our society will be more ecologically minded.

The population will grow steadily across the nation; there will be a return to the fields, and migration will become a thing of the past. People will work where they were born, near their families, immersed in their customs and culture. No one will be forced from their homeland by hunger and poverty.

Wealth will be more evenly distributed, and workers' purchasing power will have increased by at least 20 percent. We will have strengthened the internal market, and the population's needs will be met. No Mexican will go hungry, and no one will live in extreme poverty, nor will anyone be barred from education or medical care. The elderly will have decent pensions and will live without economic anxieties.

By 2024, organized crime will be greatly reduced. By then, employment and welfare policies and programs will have been successfully implemented. Young people will have no need to engage in antisocial behavior when presented with meaningful alternatives and opportunities.

Crime rates will be reduced by half; there will be fewer homicides, kidnappings, carjackings, and home invasions. Mexico shall no longer be a nation of violence, of "the disappeared," of human rights violations.

By 2024, white collar crime and political corruption will be greatly reduced. Honesty will prevail and public servants will be respected in society. Our institutions will no longer be held hostage by special interest groups, and the proper separation of powers will ensure the legitimacy of the rule of law.

By 2024, vote-buying and electoral fraud will be but distant memories. There will be free elections, and increased citizen participation will embed democratic norms in Mexican society.

By 2024, we'll have a better society, not only because of the economic development we will foster, but because we will have created a new way of thinking, a revolution in conscience that will prevent avarice, corruption, and greed from prevailing over truth, morality, and fraternity.

EPILOGUE
MIGRANTS, MOTORS OF GROWTH
Elena Poniatowska

We Mexican people hung our heads in shame when ex-president Vicente Fox declared in the 1980s that it was a source of pride that remittances from our migrants sent from the United States were the second largest source of income in our country. What most of us considered a great failure was to him a cause for celebration.

If there were work in Mexico, nobody would have left. If government functionaries had not confused public service with personal enrichment, the poorest Mexicans would not be forced to leave. If corruption had not engulfed each successive government, an income sufficient to pay for basic living expenses would be within reach of all. If, in Mexico, the minimum wage were the same as in the United States, $7.25 per hour, nobody would have to leave. The Mexican government seems to believe that a minimum wage of US$4 per day (80 pesos) is acceptable in Mexico, which is a tremendous embarrassment. If only we'd all read *Hunger: A Manifesto* by the great Martín Caparrós. It is astonishing to think that the ministers of the Supreme Court might forget Article 123 of the Constitution, which asserts that all have the right to dignified and socially useful work. What dignified work earns $4 per day? The president of the Court earns $35,457 per month—that's

$1,151 per day. Other ministers earn $27,000 per month, besides the usual slew of benefits enjoyed by Mexican functionaries.

Ex-presidents Vicente Fox, Felipe Calderón, and Luis Echeverría receive an annual pension of more than $200,000. Widows of presidents receive a pension of more than $100,000 during the first year that reduces by 10 percent each year until reaching half of the initial sum. Felipe Calderón retains the Presidential Guard as bodyguards for his family, and we all watched in awe as the mansions on "Dog Hill"[102] proliferated.

The phenomenon of mass migration from Mexico began over half a century ago. We all migrate in search of better living conditions. From Patagonia to Alaska, thousands of families have left in search of a better life. Migrants from Europe and South America once found a paradise in Mexico. A laborer from Tijuana, don Crispín, told me that fifteen years ago that his grandfather, his father, and later he himself supported themselves as gardeners in San Diego and that he was able to come and go between both countries in a matter of minutes. "Border? What border! We planted seeds, we pruned grass, we arranged rose bushes, and by 6 o'clock we were home. We traveled back and forth with ease."

The seventy-two immigrants murdered in San Fernando, Tamaulipas, Mexico in August 2010 who hailed from Central and South America are an example of the struggles faced by undocumented populations. The bodies of Hondurans, Salvadorans, Guatemalans, Brazilians, and Mexicans were piled up and left outdoors. We now know that the Zetas[103] were behind this crime.

Risking their lives, Latin Americans abandon their homes and are threatened by criminal gangs that attempt to recruit them in

---

102 President José López Portillo was accused of using the federal treasury for personal enrichment; he built a five mansion complex that came to be known as "Dog Hill" in reference to his promise to "fight like a dog" to defend the value of the peso.

103 Known as Mexico's most dangerous drug cartel (http://www.cnn.com/2009/WORLD/americas/08/06/mexico.drug.cartels.index.html).

northern Mexico or along the border. *La Bestia*[104] (also known as the Death Train) illustrates what happens when countries with few resources abandon their own. The train has now been replaced by a ship; migrants traverse the Usumacinta River and the Lacandon Jungle to reach Tenosique, Tabasco. In Tenosique, they board the train to reach Coatzacoalcos and then the border. Of course, there is less space than on the train, space enough for fifteen or twenty at most and they face great risks. The threat of drowning is ever present as smugglers charge steep fees yet treat them worse than cattle.

The too-frequent tragedy faced by those who attempt to reach "paradise" in the United States is immeasurable.

Father Alejandro Solalinde—our candidate for the Nobel Peace Prize—argues that what most concerns our government is not the plight of migrants, but the suspension of remittances. Zacatecas, among other states, relies heavily on these remittances. If they were to cease, the whole state—one of the most beautiful in the republic—would be paralyzed. As economist Jacques Rogozinski says, immigrants are always better suited to compete in the global economy because they're so eager to get ahead. "A nation of immigrants is a nation of entrepreneurs."

Today, the new president of the United States intends to build a wall between his country and ours. Already, 3,185 kilometers of one of the longest borders on earth have been fenced off in different areas with a wall so high that migrants attempting to jump it risk death. On March 24, 2017, the media announced that Trump was unable to annul Obamacare. It's possible that he will suffer another embarrassing political defeat when he is denied his wall. But perhaps his wall will be built and our grandchildren will look upon it just as travelers from around the world look at the Great Wall of China, a cultural relic of a different time.

Mexico, just like the US, is a country that has always welcomed migrants and conscientious objectors. Lázaro Cárdenas welcomed

---

104 A network of cargo trains. Migrants frequently ride the tops of these trains en route to the United States, but getting on is hugely dangerous and results in thousands of deaths per year.

Republicans from the Spanish Civil War in 1939. Before that, he welcomed Leon Trotsky and Natalia Sedova,[105] and now their grandchildren and great grandchildren are doctors, poets, and historians. Esteban Volkov, their grandson, today directs the Trotsky museum in his family's former home in Coyoacán, the same house where his grandparents protected him from assassination attempts. Their granddaughter, Patricia Volkov Fernández, is head of the Department of Infectious Diseases in the National Institute of Cancer Research. Her sister Veronica is an accomplished poet who has written brilliantly on the work of Francisco Toledo.[106] Similarly, the children of Mariana Frenk[107] and those of her siblings raised celebrated doctors such as former secretary of health Julio Frenk. The last names of some of our greatest people are many and varied in their origins. They include names like doctor Jesús Kumate, who was secretary of health from 1988–94; they also include Hungarians like Frida Kahlo; French, Irish, Czech, Roman, and German people (such as Enrique Graue Wiechers, the rector of the National Autonomous University of Mexico), as well as the incomparable doctor David Kershenobich, director of the National Institute of Health Sciences and Nutrition.

Yes, don Crispín would be hurt to know that he is no longer welcome. He never knew fear and persecution on the border, but his children and grandchildren know it intimately. They know the meaning of death, because in 2012 there were 777 deaths along the border, 652 from exposure and even from bullets from Border Patrol agents. In more recent years, unprecedentedly large numbers of the poorest Mexicans have drowned in the river. According to official data, the US deported 147,000 migrants in 2016.

The US receives more migrants than anywhere else on earth. In 2010, its population included 43 million immigrants and ten

---

105 Leon Trotsky was offered asylum in Mexico in December of 1936.

106 A Mexican sculptor, painter, and graphic artist from Oaxaca.

107 Celebrated author and translator who took residence in Mexico from her native Germany.

million undocumented migrants. In 2016, the undocumented population stood at eleven million.

Finally, I'd like to reiterate what thousands of Mexicans have been saying for twelve years: "It's an honor to support Obrador." We shall continue to stand by him because we want to live in safety, and we want the Mexican people to sleep with food in their bellies. If AMLO is able to close the gap between rich and poor, he will be a great president. Nothing is as important as awakening the people's conscience through love, education, and health. When *Peje*[108] says "first, the poor," he speaks not only to the Mexican people but to all those who transit through Mexico, all those migrants who have risked their lives navigating "La Bestia" and the Usumacinta River.

108 An affectionate nickname for López Obrador.

ABOUT THE AUTHOR

Newly elected president of Mexico Andrés Manuel López Obrador was Head of Government of the Federal District (Mexico City) from 2000 to 2005. He resigned to run as a candidate in the 2006 and 2012 presidential elections, representing a coalition led by the Party of the Democratic Revolution (PRD). He is today the leader and founder of the National Regeneration Movement (MORENA).